I WASN'T BORN ———————
BULLETPROOF

Lessons I've Learned (So You Don't Have To)

MACI BOOKOUT

A POST HILL PRESS BOOK

I Wasn't Born Bulletproof:
Lessons I've Learned (So You Don't Have To)
© 2017 by Maci Bookout
All Rights Reserved

ISBN: 978-1-68261-323-8
ISBN (eBook): 978-1-68261-324-5

Cover Photography by Tyler Andrews, tylerandrews.com
Interior Design and Composition, Greg Johnson/Textbook Perfect

Post Hill Press
New York • Nashville
posthillpress.com

Published in the United States of America

DEDICATION

To my husband, Taylor
For believing in me, supporting me, and loving me.
For being the best dad to our kids,
for putting up with my shit,
and for making sure there is always beer in the fridge.
You rock babe!

To Post Hill Press and Wenonah Hoye
Thank you for your editorial direction
and for making this book a reality.

To my readers
The readers who will learn something,
the readers who will love something,
and the readers who will laugh at something.
Thank you for the time you will spend reading this book.

CONTENTS

BECOMING
BULLETPROOF

The first time I stood up in front of a crowd of people I didn't know and spoke about my life was when I was just seventeen years old. *16 & Pregnant* had just aired on MTV and a guidance counselor at a local Catholic school had gotten in touch and asked me to come speak to a group of her students. Of course I said yes, but I had absolutely no idea what I was getting into.

I walked into it thinking that talking about my experience of getting pregnant at such a young age would be beneficial to these girls because I was a peer talking *with* them and not *at* them, but I quickly realized that it wasn't that simple. It was very intense because I was taking on this serious, taboo subject—especially for an all-girls Catholic school—and as soon as I started speaking I began to doubt myself. I remember standing up there on the podium, in this gym full of girls (some of whom were older than I was at the time) and immediately my confidence evaporated. To them, I was just another teenage girl and I could almost feel them judging me—everything I said, what I was wearing, my hair, my mistakes, my *life*. I spoke about my high school and my experience with relationships, the fact that I was a virgin before I met Ryan, how I got pregnant. But even as I was speaking, I could feel myself shutting down; it was like I could hear myself talking, but the words were coming from someone else.

Afterward, I realized that if I was really going to help people I had to learn not to give a damn about what anyone thought of me. What did it matter if most of them were judging me, if my truth helped even just one girl in that gym? After that I spoke at a few more local high schools, and from there, as I got a bit older, I started speaking at colleges and universities all over the country. I would share my story with the audience and often I would realize, as I was telling them about some difficult or painful experience, that I had never talked about it or shared what I had gone through with the people closest to me. By talking and writing about my life I learned to examine myself and my choices, to reflect on my actions and learn from my mistakes. Sometimes it's easier to be vulnerable with strangers than it is with the people closest to you, and once you do open up you realize that you are not alone and that people don't think of you or react to you differently. You learn to accept yourself.

I had a similar experience watching myself on the show. In stressful situations, I would shut down and then later, when the episode aired, I would watch myself and not even remember saying certain things or reacting a certain way. So by watching my actions from the outside, and having that distance and objectivity to reflect, I was able to learn and grow.

Over the years, I have gotten a lot of feedback on social media or at talks and book signings, some negative but most positive and encouraging. The comment that stands out the most is when people say to me, "You make it look so easy; you don't let anything affect you." Although I get that it was meant to be a compliment, at first this made me feel a bit defensive because nothing about my struggles has been easy. Then I realized that, although I may have helped some people who thought, "If she can do it, I can too," I wasn't revealing my whole truth. I was only showing them the Teflon exterior. I feel pain and fear and self-doubt, just like everyone else. Yes, I am strong, but I wasn't just born that way. I've taken lessons I've learned from my parents, friends, and role models and used them to rise above the challenges I've faced.

No one is born with all the answers; becoming "bulletproof" is a journey, and there certainly will be bumps along the way, but it is a path worth taking because it leads to a stronger, happier you. In this book, I share with you the wisdom and life lessons I've acquired over the years. I am by no means perfect, nor is my way necessarily the right way, but as I decided years ago, if my truth can help one person then my story is worth telling.

–Maci

Chapter 1

DECLARATION OF INDEPENDENCE

"I love to see a young girl go out and grab the world by the lapels. Life's a bitch. You've got to go out and kick ass."

—Maya Angelou

One thing you learn quickly, when you find out at the age of sixteen that you are going to be a parent, is that you can either give up on having your own life and depend on others for support, or you can work your ass off to finish school and get the education and qualifications you need to become an independent, fully-realized, adult human being. This process is really just called "growing up," but when you're a teen mom you don't have the luxury of waiting until your twenties to figure it all out.

After I found out I was pregnant, I finished out my junior year at my high school, went to summer school, and then I enrolled in an accelerated program so I could graduate before my due date. I remember walking into class on that first day in August, feeling terrified because it was an adult high school, and I was not an adult. There

My high school graduation. *From left to right:* Sharon (my mom), me, Bentley, and Leanne (my aunt/mom's sister).

were people there who had children, and kids who had gotten kicked out of regular high school—it might as well have been called Second Chance High. I was petrified because I didn't know what to expect and I was humongous. I couldn't even sit down properly because the chairs were the kind with desks attached and my belly was so huge I couldn't fit into them. I got through it and graduated on October 8th of what would have been my senior year, and then Bentley was born on October 27th.

The following January, when Bentley was about three months old, I went back to school for an associate's degree in Media Technology. One of the nicest things I hear from people who know me from *Teen Mom* is that they are impressed that I graduated high school and

Being a young mom means that we met a little early, but it also means I get to love you a little longer. Some people said that my life ended when I had a baby, but my life had just begun.
You didn't take away from my future; you gave me a new one.

–UNKNOWN

got a degree by the age of twenty-three, but I don't feel like I'm finished with my education. I plan to go back to school and get my bachelor's. I've always been taught that education, especially for a woman, is a valuable tool for achieving independence.

My mom and dad were teen parents. They were seventeen when they had my brother, Matt, twenty when they had me. After my brother was born, my mother went back to school to get her GED, and then after she had me she went back again, this time to get a degree in Business Administration. Three-and-a-half-years later, at the age of twenty-four, she had earned her bachelor's degree on the Dean's List, all while working full-time and raising two young children. If you ask her what motivated her to work so hard, she will say, "I never wanted to have to depend on anyone for anything."

Mom's college graduation, 1995. I was 4 and my brother, Matt, was 7.

My mom has always been a role model and symbol of independence for me. So whenever someone tells me that they're impressed by what I have achieved at such a young age, despite the obstacles life has thrown at me, I can't help but think I still have a lot of catching up to do compared to what my mother has accomplished. She has never let anyone or anything define her or stand in the way of her independence.

This is a value that she has instilled in my brother and me our entire lives. From the time we were in grade school, she expected us to have a certain amount of independence and to be responsible for ourselves. When I was in middle school, Matt and I rode the same bus to school. We were expected to wake ourselves up, get ready and be in the driveway at 6:42 to catch the school bus. It rarely happened that we actually missed it, but there were many mornings that we'd be sprinting down the driveway and by the time we got on that bus we'd be totally out of breath. On the rare morning that we were just late enough to see the bus driving off, Matt and I would play rock-paper-scissors to decide who would tell mom. Somehow, it was always me that lost and I'd have to make the dreaded trek back up the driveway to the house to wake mom up and tell her we didn't get on the bus.

"One thing!" she'd say, fuming as she'd grab her car keys and throw her coat on over her pajamas, "I expect you to do one thing for yourselves and that's get on that bus." We would pile in her jeep and she'd pull out of our driveway like NASCAR, chase down that school bus, and get the driver to pull over and let us on. We'd get on that bus with our heads down, totally humiliated, but absolutely determined *never* to be late again. She's a force, our mom, and I am grateful to have

> "*I think the girl who is able to earn her own living and pay her own way should be as happy as anybody on earth. The sense of independence and security is very sweet.*"
>
> –SUSAN B. ANTHONY

had her as my role model for how to be a strong independent woman—not to mention a fierce mother.

Learning to support yourself (financially and emotionally) is fundamental to achieving any kind of success. When it comes down to it, you only have yourself to fall back on, so to thrive in the world it's important to be able to handle whatever life throws at you on your own. But, being independent is not something that comes naturally to everyone. I've watched so many people around me go from being dependent on their parents to being dependent on their partner, without ever developing the life skills necessary to stand on their own two feet.

Just like no one is born bulletproof, no one comes into this world independent; it's a collection of skills that must be learned. The younger you start the easier it will be, but it's never too late to teach and old dog how to be independent.

LIFE LESSONS

According to a **Bank of America Better Money Habits poll** of 18- to 26-year-olds, 39% said finally achieving **financial independence** is what would make them an adult. When asked what they wish they had learned more about in school:

- 43% said they wished they had learned how to **invest**;
- 40%, said how to **do taxes**;
- 26%, said how to **manage monthly bills**;
- 21%, said how to **save for retirement**.

Source: time.com

Oh Captain, My Captain

True independence begins with being secure in who you are and in what you believe. It is much more beneficial to listen to the voice inside you than to allow yourself to be influenced by others. Being in control of your own life and your own choices can be terrifying, but it is also empowering. Remember: when you are the captain of your own ship, *you* are in control of the destination.

All too often we make the mistake of relying on others to make us happy, but this kind of dependency can be fatal to a relationship. The truth is: No one can make you happy. Putting your happiness in the hands of a significant other, thinking this will bring you fulfillment, is not

"Who needs a man when you can load your own dirt bike onto the truck?"

only misguided, you are more than likely becoming a burden to your partner who in reality cannot "complete you." Learning to find happiness within yourself, will not only make you stronger, but it also will prevent you from repeating a pattern of staying in dysfunctional relationships because you are afraid of being on your own.

Trust Your Instincts

The road to independence is paved with decisions you have made on your own. It's one thing to ask your friends to weigh in on your outfit of the day, but do you really need to consult with the group on every decision you have to make? *Is it time for a career change? Should I end things once and for all with my on-again-off-again boyfriend? Would I look good with bangs?* These are questions only *you* can answer, and looking to others to make those choices for you could have disastrous consequences—the least of which is having to spend six months growing out your hair.

Party of One

A big part of being independent is being comfortable with yourself, but when was the last time you went to a movie or out to eat on your own, or just spent some quiet time in your own head. Being *on your own* is not the same thing as being *alone*. Spend time with yourself. Enjoy your own company—after all, if you don't why should anyone else?

REASONS TO BE MORE INDEPENDENT

1. **Independence = self-esteem.** When you believe in your capacity to deal with any challenge and trust yourself to be competent in the situations you confront, it will increase your self-esteem. A boost in self-esteem, in turn, gives you a more positive outlook on life.

2. **Don't be a burden.** If you are capable of meeting your own needs, you will never have to depend on anyone else for help.

3. **Helping others.** It is not bad to need help—everyone needs it at some point—but with independence comes the ability to care for yourself and the people around you. People learn to trust you and look to you for help, instead of the other way around.

4. **Financial freedom.** Having the skills to work and earn a salary that allows you to provide for yourself and prepare for the future is critical to overall happiness in life. If you depend on another person for financial support it gives that person power over you. Financial uncertainty is frightening; financial independence is empowering.

5. **Social independence.** The key to healthy friendships is a balance of give and take. Being a socially independent person means letting go of relationships that drain you and surrounding yourself with people with whom you have mutually supportive relationships.

The true value of independence is that it leads to freedom and sustained happiness. If you are dependent on another person (whether it's a family member, a romantic partner, or a friend) you create a debt with that person and you give them power over your life. The debt that dependency creates doesn't just have to be financial. You can be financially independent, but socially and emotionally dependent on other people. Breaking free of that debt and becoming truly independent is hard work, but the benefit is measured in the freedom to pursue your own happiness.

Chapter 2

WITH A LITTLE HELP FROM MY FRIENDS...

"A day without friendship is like a pot without a single drop of honey."

−WINNIE THE POOH

The first time I understood the meaning of true friendship was when I confided to my closest friends that I was pregnant. Long after I had come to terms with my pregnancy in my own life, I struggled with the idea of telling my friends at school. I knew I could take care of myself and my baby, but I couldn't stand the idea of anyone passing judgment on me, feeling pity for me, or reducing me to a statistic. So I waited as long as possible to tell anyone outside of my family.

At sixteen, I was an athlete, I was popular, I worked hard in school and got good grades (except for math)— girls like me just didn't get "knocked up." I was a part of a tight-knit group of girlfriends, most of whom I'd known since elementary school, and the seven of us had been inseparable since freshman year. We always said we'd be best friends forever, but it wasn't until I confided to them

The girls threw me a baby shower for Bentley. (*From left to right:* Me, Rebecca, Lauren, Sway, Mimi, and Keelie.)

that I was pregnant that I really *knew* it was true. I had no idea how they would react, but when I finally told Sway, Keelie, Lauren, Brittany, Rebecca, and Mimi—after they got over the initial shock—to my surprise and relief they were all unconditionally supportive.

Even after I made the decision to leave our high school, so I could graduate before the baby came, they stood by me. They came to support me at my graduation, threw me a baby shower, and on the day Bentley was born they left school early to come visit me in the hospital. It

Top: The girls at
my bedside, the day
Bentley was born.
Bottom: The girls at the
beach, Lauren, Sway,
Brittany, Rebecca,
Keelie, and me.

wasn't just the big things either. I remember this one time
when I was about six months pregnant, Rebecca's mother
took all of us for a weekend trip to the beach. After we
had settled in, the girls let me nap while her mom went
to the grocery store to pick up food for all of us. Without
my knowing, they had filled her in on my pregnancy
cravings and when I woke up starving, the fridge was
filled with stacks of pizza Lunchables and two huge bags
of whole radishes (I've always loved radishes but when

I was pregnant with Bentley I ate them by the fistful). I will never forget moments like that. While we were on that trip, I had a little baby bump and we took individual pictures of each of them kissing my belly. After Bentley was born I had the photos framed and they hung on the wall in his room, like seven sweet angels watching over him in his crib.

When I needed it most, Sway, Keelie, Lauren, Brittany, Rebecca, and Mimi stood by me; they made sure that I knew they loved me and that I was still an important member of our circle of friends. Because of their friendship, I learned that it's okay to be vulnerable and ask for help, and that often with true friends you won't even have to ask.

The Golden Rule

Always be the type of friend that you would like to have. Don't keep score, and never do things expecting a return. If you trust the friendship, your investment will come back to you tenfold. This may seem like common sense, but if your most precious relationships are built on this

> "Friendship is the hardest thing in the world to explain. It's not something you learn in school. But if you haven't learned the meaning of friendship, you really haven't learned anything."
> —MUHAMMAD ALI

simple yet solid principal, they will last a lifetime.

LIFE LESSONS

A **10-year study by the Centre for Ageing** at Flinders University in Australia found that **a supportive network of friends** is actually more important than close family relatives in prolonging life. People **over the age of 70** with an extensive network of friends tended to **live 22% longer** than those with fewer friends.

Source: executivestyle.com

24K Friends

When Bentley was a newborn, waking up for feedings every night, Keelie—who I now refer to as The Baby Whisperer—would come and stay the night with me and get up with him so I could get some desperately needed sleep. I never asked for her help, but she gave it without hesitation. She was a senior in high school, she could have been out on a date or at a party, but she *chose* to be with me and my crying baby. But, more than that, she never held it against me, or made me feel that I owed her anything in return. I was going through such a difficult adjustment and for her to be there for me so selflessly, that's when it truly hit home that real friends are important to have and to keep in your life. Like any relationship, you have to work at it, but true friends are worth their weight in gold.

That next year, while my girlfriends were applying to college, going to parties, and doing all the things that typical high school seniors do, I was adjusting to life with a newborn. I was still a teenager, but I became an adult overnight, and while my friends' biggest concerns were getting a date for prom and deciding what cute outfit they were going to wear to Friday night's football game, I was up to my eyeballs in bills, poopy diapers, and baby spew.

In the fall, Sway, Keelie, Lauren, Brittany, Rebecca, and Mimi all went off to college. Sway went to Mt. Holyoke and Mimi went to Kennesaw State for the first year, but after that they all went to Middle Tennessee State University. Sway and Mimi lived together in an apartment, Lauren and Rebecca roomed together in a dorm, and Keelie and Brittany lived in an apartment complex on campus. If I hadn't gotten pregnant with Bentley I probably would have followed them to MTSU, but that would have been more about me being a teenager and wanting to be with my friends. Eventually, I would have realized that I wanted to do something completely different on my own, but at the time I definitely felt a sense of *Oh, shit. If they're all gone, who am I gonna hang out with*?

At this point, it would have been totally understandable if we had just quietly drifted apart, but whenever they came home for break they made a point to come visit me or I would take Bentley to the MTSU campus and visit them on quiet weekends. Even though everything was working against us, we made the effort to keep our friendship going and ten years later the seven of us are

"How many slams in an old screen door? Depends how loud you shut it. How many slices in a bread? Depends how thin you cut it. How much good inside a day? Depends how good you live 'em. How much love inside a friend? Depends how much you give 'em."

–Shel Silverstein

all still close. We see each other regularly (some of them I see once or twice a week), and we have a group text message that has been going for years. A few of the girls have moved away, but when we see each other it's like no time has passed.

When we were in high school, nobody took our friendship seriously. So just for shits and giggles and to irritate anybody that we didn't like, we named ourselves SYD and came up with our own secret hand symbol (thumb and pointer together with three fingers in the air, like the "okay" sign) that we always made in group photos.

For years people would ask us what SYD meant and we would tell them it was a secret—but really we just couldn't come up with a cool name. Eventually, we started telling people that SYD stood for "Seclude Yourself Daily," but the initials actually came from "Suzuki-Yamaha of Dalton" and this one memorable night during sophomore year that we drove through a rainstorm to meet up with a couple of boys we liked. One of the boy's parents ran a motorcycle dealership forty minutes away in Dalton, Georgia. We met up with them there and snagged a bunch of T-shirts and swag with the SYD logo before racing home to beat curfew. I remember it was raining so hard it was like driving through a monsoon, but we hauled ass and made it back without our parents ever finding out we had crossed the state line to flirt with boys. The initials stuck and to this day, we are still the SYD girls and any time one of us gets married or has a baby we have SYD bridal and baby showers.

LIFE LESSONS

Having a **close circle of friends** can be good for your health. Research suggests that strong social ties may help **stave off memory loss** as you age; **reduce stress**; **boost immunity**; help you **lose weight** and keep it off; and, **buffer against depression**. A 2010 review of nearly 150 studies that was published in *PLoS Medicine* found that people with strong social ties had a **50% better chance of survival**, regardless of age, sex, health status, and cause of death, than those with weaker ties.

Source: Huffington Post, April 2014

The seven of us all have completely different personalities and interests, and if we met now we might not be such good friends, but because we've known each other for so long we are bonded by our shared history. We were there for each other's first boyfriends, first cigarettes, first heartbreaks, when we got our driver's licenses, and lost our virginity. We've kept notes that we wrote to each other in middle school and it's not uncommon for one of us to dig up embarrassing photos from middle school and blow them up for bachelorette or birthday parties. Having that kind of history around you is very grounding.

Social Skills

After eight years of dealing with tabloid reporters showing up at my work digging around for something juicy to print, or having people latch onto me because they think my name will get them on the right list at some club or event, I can meet someone and within the first five minutes I will know if they're interested in being friends with *me* or the benefits of being around someone who's on television.

But, in the beginning I didn't have that skill. I've always been friendly and open to meeting new people, so in order not to be taken advantage of I had to learn to quickly assess people's character and capacity. (This is actually an important skill to develop when you become a parent as well, because you just don't have that kind of time to waste on pointless people anymore.) Beware of would-be users and opportunists trying to hitch themselves to your friendship wagon. Developing skills for assessing the intentions of the people around you will not only protect you from being taken advantage of, it will enhance the relationships you already have because you will know that they are built on a solid foundation.

Types of Friends

Although nothing can take the place of a besty who will be there for you in your deepest, darkest hour, not every friend can be your ride-or-die—nor is it realistic to expect that. As I've gotten older and matured I've learned that there are many different types of friends—some you want in your life, others you should avoid at all costs. The trick is recognizing a person's friendship capacity and then deciding if he or she makes sense in your life.

The Toxic Friend

Whether they are dragging you down when they're miserable or encouraging your worst inclinations, the Toxic Friend will bring nothing but negativity into your life. This type of friend wants you to feel their insecurities and to live in their misery. They bring out the worst in you and then revel in watching you unravel. Your joy somehow takes away from theirs, so they can never genuinely be happy for you. Think of the Toxic Friend like a bad habit you need to break (like smoking, or habitually checking your Twitter feed).

The Drama Queen

Ever notice that drama seems to surround certain friends? If they're not fighting with their boyfriends, they're in a crisis at work, or talking shit behind another friend's back. They stir up drama so they can feed off the attention they get from the people around them. If you have someone in your life who makes you feel like—when you're together—it's more of a therapy session than a friendship, then you have found your very own Drama Queen.

The Childhood Friend

If you are lucky enough to make it to your twenties with a friend—or better yet *friends*—that you've known from childhood, hang on tight and never let go. Your Childhood Friend knew you back when and will remind you of who you are and where you came from. There's nothing quite so grounding as having a friend who can bust out a photo from back when you had braces and bad hair.

LIFE LESSONS

Several studies have shown that, at least between chimpanzees, baboons, horses, hyenas, elephants, bats, and dolphins, animals can form friendships for life with individuals that aren't from their species.

Source: Huffington Post, April 2014

The Girls' Night Out Friend

When you want a legitimate night out—one where you plan in advance to take a cab home because you know you're going to drink more than you should—The Girls' Night Out Friend is the perfect companion. They can be coworkers or close friends, but their one essential quality is that they are totally down to go to the Waffle House at 3:00 a.m. because they don't have anyone or anything to worry about in the morning.

The Long-Distance Friend

There are two kinds of Long-Distance Friends: the ones who are geographically far away and the ones who live nearby but you can still go months without seeing them. I have both kinds of Long-Distance Friends and I cherish them all deeply. It can be difficult for some to see the value in a friend you only see once or twice a year. It's easy to think, *If they're not texting me, calling, or making an effort to see me every day, this person must not care about me.* But the Long-Distance Friendship does not require this kind of daily reassurance. These friends are special because when you do reconnect, the time apart or the miles between you melt away. This person knows you so well they catch up in a beat and dispense advice with laser accuracy. You have to trust and value the

Long-Distance Friendship enough to know that you don't have to see or speak to each other every day to know that person is going to be there for you when it matters most.

The Mommy Friend

Now that I'm a mother of three, my Mommy Friends are an absolutely essential part of my life. When Bentley was a baby, I didn't have any friends who had children. I was young, but I was still a single mom and I needed someone to relate to and bounce my experiences off of. It was hard to talk about relationships with my non-Mommy Friends because the stakes were higher for me. If their boyfriends did something stupid they could just kick them to the curb, but I always have to put my children's needs first. Mommy Friends get that.

With Mommy Friends, you can plan to do fun things with your kids, which has the added bonus of creating lifelong friendships for your children (*and* you save money on a babysitter!). Another great thing about Mommy Friends: it's fun to go out *without* your children. You say you're not going to talk about the kids, but half the time you do anyway and some of the best stuff to talk about is making fun of your kids. Only other moms understand that when complain about your children, you are complaining with love.

The Besty

Last but not least, the beloved Besty. Although it may be the most overused friendship hashtag on the Internet, it is also the most important kind of friend. Your Besty is the one you *don't* have to call when the shit hits the fan ('cause she's already right there by your side, helping you mop up the mess). Your Besty tells you straight up when you look like shit, or when you're being a bitch. Your Besty listens to *all* your bullshit. She'll hold your hair back when you puke, or blow off a date to eat ice cream and binge-watch *The Walking Dead* with you on a Friday night. A Besty makes you laugh so hard snot comes out your nose. If you don't already have one, I highly recommend you reexamine your social priorities.

It's Not Me, It's You

Breaking up is never easy, but it's even harder when it's a friend that you need to end things with. A few years ago, I befriended a girl who was dating a guy that I had known my whole life. He also happened to be good friends with my boyfriend at the time, so we hung out together as couples a lot. After a while I started to notice that drama always seemed to surround her. She could be passive aggressive and manipulative, and I was always catching her in some lie or another. Her friends, myself included, were always getting dragged into her drama—without us necessarily understanding what we were getting into. Her relationship with her boyfriend was unhealthy; they were always fighting and if she was having an issue with him she would make out like it was *all* of our boyfriends.

> "Lots of people want to ride with you in the limo, but what you want is someone who will take the bus with you when the limo breaks down."
> –OPRAH WINFREY

I sensed this about her early on and, though I tried to give her the benefit of the doubt, eventually it got to the point where I knew I needed to confront her. So one day, I finally sat down with her and explained gently but firmly how I was feeling. She was emotional, but she wasn't defensive. I realized that, on some level, she wasn't even aware that she had been doing these things. She seemed to really take in what I had to say and I was hopeful that things would improve.

As time went on, though, nothing changed and within six months it became clear that this was really just who she was and, at this point in her life at least, she wasn't capable of change. I had two choices: continue to put up with her negative presence in my life, or break up with her. It was difficult to do and, even though it was a relief not to be dragged into her drama anymore, for a while I felt guilty because I couldn't point to a specific reason that I wanted to end our friendship.

In some ways breaking up with a friend is harder than breaking up with a boyfriend, because you will always feel like a failure. By definition of being a friend you feel like you should be there No Matter What. But, finally I realized it's okay to break ties with a person in your life who isn't healthy for you.

How you handle the breakup is going to depend on the specifics of the friendship and the situa-

> *"A friend is one that knows you as you are, understands where you have been, accepts what you have become, and still, gently allows you to grow."*
>
> –WILLIAM SHAKESPEARE

tion, but the most important thing to remember is that it is far better to be honest than to allow negative feelings to fester. In this case, I was honest about my feelings and I made clear what my limitations were. She got the message and eventually our friendship settled into a place I was comfortable with. The most important thing when you find yourself in an unhealthy friendship is that you communicate to the other person what your issues are.

On the Other Hand...

If you are going to dish it out, you also have to be the type of person who is willing to receive criticism. My very best friends know that if I do something they don't like, they can call me on it and I will listen. I won't be offended and it won't lead to a crazy argument. True friendship is based on this kind of trust and openness: to listen to the things you don't always want to hear.

Chapter 3

INSIDE AND OUT

Whether it's through words, clothing, hairstyle, or art forms such as writing or drawing, personal expression is how we display our individuality and share our true spirit and character with the outside world. If you have fully embraced your personal expression, the people around you will see the person you are on the inside shining through. While, it's not always easy to do, expressing one's "self" fully is essential to attaining peace, happiness, and fulfillment.

Personal expression has always been an important part of my identity. I've always been a bit rebellious, and like a lot of teenagers I expressed that aspect of my personality through fashion. In high school, I was always a bit edgier than my girlfriends; I wore black converse, black nail polish, and my ears were gauged. But my need to stand out from the crowd and express my individuality began when I was even younger, and there were times when being true to myself came with consequences.

In the spring of 5th grade I tried out for the middle school cheer team. It was a very competitive team and I ended up being one of only two incoming 6th graders who made the cut. Going into it that fall I had no idea how much being on the team would impact my social life, but I quickly learned that being a cheerleader elevated my social status and made it easy

"The most important kind of freedom is to be what you really are."
    –JIM MORRISON

for me to make friends and be liked be everybody. Even back then, my sense of style was "edgier" than most of the other girls around me, so I wasn't exactly what you would consider a stereotypical cheerleader, but I liked being popular so I reigned in my style so I would fit in.

When I tried out for the team again at the end of that year and this time didn't make the cut, I was devastated—not because I loved cheering so much, but because I was worried what everyone would think and how it would affect me socially. I remember that whole year I had been begging my mom for a pair of Converse or Etnies (which, at the time, were a popular skate shoe, like DC), but my mom wouldn't get them for me. She knew that I wouldn't wear them often enough to justify the expense because they didn't fit with the cheer team "look." On the day I found out that I didn't make the team for 7th grade, she came home with a pair of pink Converse she had picked up for me at Dick's to cheer me up. That's when I began to understand that I had been suppressing my personal expression just to fit in and be popular, and I vowed never to let that happen again.

Never one to give up in the face of failure, at the end of that year I tried out for the cheer team again and this time I made the cut. 8th grade was all about competitions, pep rallies, and school events. This time I was much more laid

"Don't you ever let a soul in the world tell you that you can't be exactly who you are."

–LADY GAGA

back about the experience because I head learned that I didn't *need* to be on the team to make friends, and best of all, I had decided to just be *me*. So when my coach approached me about my black nail polish, I told her respectfully, "I was pretty much born wearing black nail polish. Everybody knows that about me. It's a part of who I am." But she wasn't having it. She told me that if I didn't take the polish off for the football game that night she was going to make me sit for the entire game. Honestly, I did consider taking it off—nobody wants to work that hard and then not be allowed to participate—but I decided that it was important to be true to myself, no matter the consequences I might face.

So that night, I went to the game with my nails painted black as always. The coach sat me for the first quarter, but then she gave in and let me cheer for the rest of the game. I stood my ground and I felt like she respected me for it (although, to be honest, she probably only put me back in because the lines in our cheer formations would have been uneven if I were missing).

My Body Is My Canvas...

Body art is a deeply personal and controversial form of personal expression. There are many people out there who consider tattoos a sin because it's "marking" your body. While I respect that view, I believe it's no different than piercing your ears or dying your hair. That said, I would never encourage anyone to get a tattoo. It is a personal choice that should not be made lightly. Remember: ink on paper fades, but ink on skin is forever.

Believe it or not, my tattoos are something that I have always kept very private. My goal has never been to show them off; a lot of people don't

> *"My body is my journal, and my tattoos are my story."*
> –JOHNNY DEPP

even know I have my whole back done. My tattoos are an expression of my faith: faith in myself, faith in my family, and faith in God. They are small reminders of my story, lessons that have had an impact on my identity and my journey.

However, there have been moments where I wasn't so sure my body art should take center stage. When Taylor and I were planning our wedding, I considered covering them up. I didn't want people staring at my tattoos instead of paying attention to the ceremony. When I told Taylor he said, "No. They are part of who you are and what I love about you." This was a great reminder for me that my tattoos aren't just decorative, they represent my journey—who I was and who I am. To cover them up for such an important moment in my life would not have been true to myself and I am blessed to have a partner who values the importance of my personal expression.

LIFE LESSONS

According to **The Harris Poll** of 2,225 US adults surveyed online from October 14–19, 2015:

- **Tattoos** are especially **popular among younger Americans**, with nearly half of Millennials (47%) and more than a third of Gen Xers (36%) saying they have at least one, compared to 13% of Baby Boomers and one in ten Matures (10%).
- **Millennials and Gen Xers** (37% and 24%) are also exponentially more likely than their elders (6% Baby Boomers, 2% Matures) to have **multiple tattoos**.
- A third (33%) of inked adults indicate having a tattoo has made them **feel sexy**. Roughly a third also say that it makes them **feel attractive** (32%), though it's worth noting that this percentage has grown considerably from 21% in 2012.
- Just over a quarter (27%) say it makes them feel more **rebellious** and two in ten (20%) feel more **spiritual** as a result of their tattoos.

Source: theharrispoll.com

A Map of Me

Over the years, a lot of people have asked me about the significance of my tattoos. Each one is deeply meaningful to me. I think of them as pieces of my puzzle. Each one is different, but all together they add up to me. I love them, and I don't give a damn if anyone else approves.

Bulletproof was my first tattoo. It is such a simple word, but it's meaning has such power and significance in my life. I had this placed on the back of my right shoulder as a reminder to myself that no matter the struggle I happen to face in life, nothing can ever break my spirit.

After that, I had my son's name, **Bentley Cadence**, inked in purple script on the back of my left hip. We had chosen the name Bentley before I even knew whether I was having a boy or girl. Cadence came to me one day while I was sitting in my junior-year English Lit class. I was going over some vocabulary words and came across the meaning for the word "cadence," which refers to the rhythmic sequence or flow of sounds in language. It made me think of the pattern in my own life of my mother and father being teen parents, and I felt this word was a beautiful expression of that repetition in our lives.

I have since had **Jayde Carter** added in the same script (but in teal with black outline) to the back of my right hip—directly across from the "Bentley Cadence" tattoo. I love the deep meaning and the simplicity of the style of these tattoos. In my opinion, they are the prettiest ones I have. Eventually, I will add **Maverick Reed** in the same font somewhere on my back. From the moment I found out I was pregnant with Bentley, my life was forever changed. My children are my light and my joy, and these tattoos represent the strength I have found in my journey as a mother.

Starting right below my left breast, then across my ribs, and going all the way to my spine is the phrase **Learn to Feel**. The placement was strategically thought out, considering it's on one of the most painful places to be tattooed. I had this tattoo done when I was going through a very dark and emotional period in my life. At the time, as a self-defense mechanism, I had become completely numb to my feelings and emotions, but eventually I realized that in order to push through the struggle I would have to "learn to feel" before I could let go of the pain. This tattoo is a reminder never to cut myself off from my emotions, no matter how painful they may be.

The first tattoo I got on my back is of a piece of well-used **notebook paper**. It literally covers my entire back and represents my passion for writing. Written diagonally in script across the paper are a few lines of a poem that I wrote when I was nineteen:

> *When my heart hurts worse than my head,*
> *that is when i will get scared...*
> *and that is when i will know,*
> *that it is worth it all.*

Close to the bottom of the notebook paper is my last name. The three Os in "Bookout" are replaced with cupcakes representing my mom, dad, and brother. The cupcakes come from the fact that when I was younger I used to love to bake. In fact, for a long time it was my dream to go to culinary school. As a kid I was always making cupcakes, to the point where if we didn't have any in the house my dad and brother would come home and be like, "Where are the cupcakes?"

Across my left shoulder I have a tattoo of an **anatomical heart**. This is my most personal tattoo and I've never shared its significance with anyone.

On my right shoulder, under Bulletproof is a beautiful tattoo of a **pocket watch**, the hands of which point to the hour and minute that I was born. Someday, I plan to add a script that says, "Timing is everything, even if it's not on purpose."

On my right forearm, I have a very realistic tattoo of a **#2 pencil**; it literally looks like there is a pencil resting on my arm. This significance of this tattoo is simply that I love to write, and as odd as it may sound in this age of texting and technology, I prefer to write using a pencil. Writing can be a very powerful form of personal expression, and I consider the pencil to be my "weapon of choice."

Future Ink

For my next tattoo, I plan to get my whole arm done. I've always wanted to get a spiritual tattoo and plan to have a sleeve done using the symbol of the dandelion flower.

The dandelion is considered to be God's flower because it never dies. It has three phases that are equivalent to the sun, the moon, and the stars. The first phase is the yellow flower: the sun. In the second phase, the bloom is replaced by a round, white poof of seeds: the moon. The third phase occurs when these seeds are blown into the wind and the flower is reborn: the stars. No matter what I go through, I always try to be better, stronger, smarter and to me the dandelion and its phases are a powerful symbol of the evolution we all go through in life. Everything that happens to us (our struggles and our joys) contributes to our growth and makes us who we are.

I plan to have the phases inked in a spiral around my arm along with the phases of the sun, moon and stars. It's rare that people see all of my tattoos because they are on my back and shoulders so I usually have them covered. I like the idea of having a visible tattoo on my arm as a way to share my spirituality and faith with others without being too preachy or aggressive about it.

LIFE LESSONS

In the top right corner of the notebook paper **tattoo on my back**, there is a **yellow rubber duck**, identical to the one used in the *Teen Mom* logo. Being on MTV has been a huge part of my life. For good or bad, it has shaped who I am today and this is my way of honoring that experience.

Home Is Where the Art Is

About six months before we got married, Taylor and I bought our dream house. Before that we had been living in a series of places that never really felt like home to us. For a while we were renting this tiny place that we called the "Love Shack Mansion" because it was tiny (two small bedrooms, a tiny kitchen and living room, and one bathroom), and super old and run down (the floors and most of the cabinets and appliances were from the 80s—maybe even the 70s). When we found out I was pregnant with Jayde, we rushed into buying a place because we knew we needed more space to accommodate our growing family. The house was in a decent neighborhood with a nice-sized yard, but it didn't feel like our forever home. If I hadn't gotten pregnant with Maverick we might still be there, but we never really decorated or did anything to the house because deep down we knew we weren't going to live there for a long time. But, once we swelled to a family of five practically overnight, we realized that we needed to set down some serious roots.

> "I am a canvas of my experiences, my story is etched in lines and shading, and you can read it on my arms, my legs, my shoulders, and my stomach."
>
> –KAT VON D

As luck would have it, a house that we had looked at the year before (but which needed way more work than we were able to take on at that point) was put back on the market, and the best part was that it was just up the street from my mom and dad's—we could literally wave to one another from the driveway. The people we bought the house from did a great job with the renovation, so all we really had to do is make it our "own." It's still a work in progress, but my two favorite rooms are the open kitchen (because I love to cook and have my friends and children around me when I do) and the cozy little room next to it, which we turned into our family den. Decorating this room was a lot of fun because everything in it, from the art on the walls to the furniture, is a reflection of who Taylor and I are. More than any other room in this house, this is *our* room. It's where we get to be parents *and* have fun. So in keeping with that spirit, we've decorated it with things that remind us who we are as individuals, as a couple, and as parents.

In the entryway from the kitchen are a couple of high stools and fun table with a pedestal made from a vintage leather golf bag that my brother and Megan, his girlfriend of eight years, gave us for Christmas. The centerpiece of the room is a small bar for entertaining that we picked up from Home Goods. Above the bar is a large aerial photograph of Neyland Stadium, home of our favorite football team, the Tennessee Volunteers. We try to get to a game at least once a year, but we'd go to every game if we could. Since we can't get out to the stadium as much as we'd like, one of our closest friends gave us this canvas print for a wedding gift as a way of bringing the stadium to us.

My favorite piece in the room has to be the quirky table that I picked up from Southeastern Salvage, a local liquidation store for furniture and building materials. It's one of those places I go every couple of weeks, just to look around. You find the coolest and weirdest stuff there. One day, I was in there just poking around and I found this piece that was made out of the front grill of a vintage Jeep, the headlights even still work. They actually had two of them and I loved it so much, I had them hold the other one for Matt and Megan.

Hands down, Taylor's favorite thing in the room is the Golden Tee virtual golf game that I gave to him as a Father's Day gift. It's the kind of arcade game they have at sports bars like Buffalo Wild Wings. Taylor and his buddies love this game, and used to play it all the time, but once we had Maverick it got more and more difficult to get out. I went on the website and it turned out they were having a Father's Day special, so I surprised Taylor with his very own Golden Tee.

Peppered around the room are framed photos, sports trophies, and small meaningful and fun knickknacks, like the faux bronzed hand making the "SYD" sign that my girlfriends gave me to celebrate our friendship. Lauren, who's got a great eye for interior design, helped me pick out the window treatments and this really cool ivory colored cowhide rug with gold flecks—I never would have bought it on my own, but it adds a really fun accent to the space and ties all the quirky elements in the room together.

Now that we have three young kids, we can't go out with our friends as much as we used to, so a lot of the time they come to us and we all hang out together with our kids in the family den, watching football and playing games. Like my mom always says, "If you can't beat 'em, join 'em." Honestly, it ain't easy being in your twenties and having three children. Most people our age—even the married ones—have a lot more

"Your home should tell the story of who you are, and be a collection of what you love."
—Nate Berkus, Interior Designer

freedom than Taylor and I do. I wouldn't change a thing about my life, but I do like to have fun and hang out with friends, so this room is a reflection of that side of who Taylor and I are.

The Healing Power of Art

Have you ever read a poem, listened to a song, or looked at a painting that perfectly captured something you had experienced or felt at some point in your life? Art is an incredibly powerful form of personal expression. It's a universal language that transcends time and cultural barriers. Whether or not you consider yourself an "artist," tapping into your creative force to give voice to your inner life can be both fun and therapeutic. For some that may come in the form of playing music or painting, while for others writing is how they best express themselves. Whatever medium is right for you, the point is to take the beauty or pain within you and give it a life outside of your mind.

Finding My Space

I first started writing as a form of personal expression when I was about fourteen years old. At the time Myspace was the big social media platform that people were using. My favorite thing about it was that you could customize your profile. I found myself always wanting to change my profile to make it very personal and specific to me. One week it would be just a typical upbeat profile, the next week I would change it to be darker or more emotional. My profile became an expression of what I was feeling at that particular moment. That's when I began to be attracted to words and their meanings.

I started carrying around a journal and was always scribbling in it. It wasn't about the satisfaction of having other people read or praise what I was writing; it was about the release putting my thoughts into words gave me. After I was done writing a poem, I would realize that I'd been sitting there for hours. It was almost like talking to a friend. That's when I realized writing had become a therapeutic form of self-expression for me.

- **Always keep a journal on hand.** Writing is a muscle and you can build its strength by exercising it regularly. Keep a journal in your purse or backpack, and whenever you have a quiet moment jot down phrases or ideas as they come into your head.

- **Read as much as possible.** A little-known secret about writers: they read. Reading actual books (and not just Twitter or Buzzfeed) will not only open your mind, on a practical level it will expand your vocabulary.

- **Use pen and paper.** Take a step back from your screen and try using good old-fashioned pen and paper. There's something very satisfying about building a poem or story without the help of autocorrect or the delete button.

- **Find a quiet time and space.** Try to set aside a regular time to write. It doesn't have to be every day, but sticking to a schedule will help you build your writing stamina.

- **Set the tone.** For some listening to music can help set the mood, for other's silence is a must. Get to know what puts you in a writing mood and then use that for inspiration.

LIFE LESSONS

According to studies conducted by James W. Pennebaker, a social psychologist and the leading researcher on the power of writing and journaling for healing purposes, **expressive writing** can improve **control over pain**, **depressed mood**, and **pain severity**. His findings suggest that expressing anger may be helpful for individuals suffering from chronic pain, particularly if it leads to **meaning making**.

Source: ncbi.nlm.nih.gov

She can hear the whispers
even in the silence

She may have asked for this
who knew it would be so violent

In a world with no privacy
she keeps so much quiet

Just a handful of thoughts
quickly becomes a riot

If everyone else knew
exactly what she thought

She wonders if she'd still be loved
or fall and never be caught

Expressing myself through writing taught me to articulate my thoughts and feelings in order to better process and grow from my experiences. Whenever I am going through a particularly difficult or emotional experience, I always make time to write about it. Even though I've never shared most of my writing with other people, it has become a powerful form of personal expression for me. It's like a snapshot of who I am in that moment. I can go back and reread something I wrote years ago, and it will bring back all of the emotion from that time.

Learning to value personal expression, whether that comes in the form of a public display of your inner life or a more private reflection, will put you on the road to happiness and inner peace.

Chapter 4

CAREER GOALS

"Do you motivate yourself with the chip on your shoulder or the love in your heart?"

–Unknown

A couple of years ago, I came across this quote online and it got me thinking that pretty much everything I do is guided by that simple concept. When you are driven by superficial goals, your accomplishments will be just as hollow. When your drive comes from love, your accomplishments will bring you true joy. Love is the greatest motivator of all.

I graduated high school through an accelerated program in October of what would have been my senior year, Bentley was born at the end of that month and then I started college the following January. In part, I pushed myself so hard because I thought it was what I was supposed to do. I felt the pressure of never wanting anyone to say that I didn't graduate high school or go to college and get a degree because I was a teen mom.

Fortunately my mom works from home and has a flexible schedule, so she was able to watch Bentley while I was waitressing at a local restaurant or at school. I spent a year working towards a degree in Business Administration, but by the end of both semesters I ended up dropping most of my classes. I was more focused on

> *"The only way to do great work is to love what you do. If you haven't found it yet, keep looking. Don't settle."*
> –STEVE JOBS

working and paying my bills, than going to class. I would think, *I can either pick up a shift or go to my Principles of Accounting class*—which would you pick?

At the end of that school year, I went to see my advisor and he told me about their Media Technology program. I had always wanted to learn more about writing and journalism, and I realized that I had been struggling, not because I had to balance work with school, but because I had no passion for what I was studying. Suddenly, instead of losing my mind in Microeconomics, I was taking classes in Film Studies, Media Law, and Radio Production. As a result, I was energized by my education and it changed my whole attitude towards going to school.

I quit my job at the restaurant and started working part time for my dad. My hours were much more flexible and I was able to focus on school, but the most important change was that I was now truly engaged and excited about what I was learning. Going to school is a lot more enjoyable when you are eager to learn and you are

> "I've come to believe that each of us has a personal calling that's as unique as a fingerprint—and that the best way to succeed is to discover what you love and then find a way to offer it to others in the form of service, working hard, and also allowing the energy of the universe to lead you."
>
> –OPRAH WINFREY

surrounded by people with common interests. I wasn't afraid to pursue my joy, and was proud that I followed my own path. Changing my major was a game changer.

After I got my Associate degree with a concentration in Media Technologies, I started working as a Social and Digital Media specialist in the marketing department of a corporation whose owner was the founder of multiple satellite businesses. It was an exciting time for me because I was able to take all the skills I had learned in school and apply them in the real world. Never in a million years would I have pictured myself happy working a nine-to-five corporate job. I have always been independent and headstrong. I thought, *There's no way I'll be able to sit in a cubicle all day and kiss my boss's ass*. But I learned from that job that all that really matters is that you love what you're doing.

"Once you realize that you have identified a passion, invest in yourself. Figure out what you need to know, what kind of experience and expertise you need to develop to do the things that you feel in your heart you will enjoy, and that will sustain you both mentally and economically."

–MARTHA STEWART

Have You Ever Seen Anyone Crying in a Porsche?

People think it makes them shallow if they admit how important money is in our lives, but let's be honest: you're gonna be a helluva lot happier if your bills are paid. You don't have to be Bill and Melinda Gates rich, but there is no question that financial stability is essential to overall happiness and a sense of wellbeing.

Now, unless you have a trust fund or a rich relative who plans to leave you a big ol' inheritance, the best way to achieve financial stability is by educating yourself (whether that means getting a degree or learning a trade is up to you). Obviously, you can't control the economy, but if you have the right skills and you set goals for yourself, you will be prepared for whatever life throws at you.

Employer or Employee?

My mom has worked for the same company for more than twenty years. She loves her job, but she also loves that at the end of the day when she turns her laptop off she can leave work behind. My father, on other hand, needs to be his own boss.

> "I'm tough, I'm ambitious, and I know exactly what I want. If that makes me a bitch, okay."
> –MADONNA

When I was a kid he ran the body shop at a car dealership. Although he was in charge, he still had people over him that he had to answer to. Deep down, he knew he'd never truly be satisfied if he was working for someone else, so about ten years ago he and my mom decided that it was time for him to open his own shop. It was a huge risk for them to take on, and it hasn't always been easy, but it was the right thing for my dad and they have never looked back.

Although the stress that comes from running your own business is intense, for some people nothing can replace the sense of pride and ownership that comes from being your own boss. On the other hand, running your own business or aggressively pursuing career advancement may not be your thing. It's essential that you know yourself and make career choices based on what will make you feel fulfilled.

LIFE LESSONS

According to *Forbes* magazine:

- There are almost **28 million small businesses** in the US.
- More than 50% of the working population (120 million individuals) works in a small business.
- Small businesses have generated more than **65% of the net new jobs** since 1995.
- Approximately 543,000 new businesses get started each month.
- The fastest growing sector for freelance businesses in 2011 included **auto repair shops**, **beauty salons**, and **dry cleaners**.

Source: Forbes.com

Things That Matter

While Taylor and I were both working at office jobs, we were presented with the opportunity to build our own apparel line. It was something Taylor had always wanted to do (I swear, if he could wear a different shirt every single day he would) so we decided to jump in with both feet.

RECIPE FOR ENTREPRENEURIAL SUCCESS

1. A dash of education.
2. A pinch of common sense.
3. A big set of balls.

Things That Matter

The name of the company TTM Lifestyle is an extension of our philosophy: *Things That Matter*. We design shirts, hoodies, and some accessories like backpacks and coffee mugs. We even did a jewelry collaboration with the Stacked Collection. Designing the graphics that appear on our clothes and collaborating with other creative people is the most fun I have ever had while working. The business took off faster than we ever expected and when I found out I was pregnant with Maverick, we realized that the income we were making would be enough for me to leave my day job and focus on the company full time. Eventually, Taylor was able to leave his job as well and now we both are able to focus on the business and work from home.

ESSENTIAL QUALITIES FOR RUNNING YOUR OWN BUSINESS

- **Discipline:** If you are going to be your own boss, you have to be the boss. You have to be accountable to the work because if you aren't, no one else will be.
- **Ambition:** A desire and determination to achieve your goals. Without ambition your dreams will stay dreams.
- **Fearlessness:** No one has ever achieved success without taking risks. If you're not willing to crack a few eggs, you probably shouldn't be baking the cake.
- **Trust in your instincts:** A successful entrepreneur must have the courage of his/her convictions.
- **Organization:** Not my strong suit, but I am learning. There are so many moving parts to running a business, that if you aren't organized you could easily overlook important details.

"If you've got an idea, start today. There's no better time than now to get going. That doesn't mean quit your job and jump into your idea 100 percent from day one, but there's always small progress that can be made to start the movement."

–KEVIN SYSTROM, COFOUNDER OF INSTAGRAM

Continuing Education

If you feel like your career is in a rut, it might be time for a new skill. Going back to school to get trained in an area that will make you invaluable to your boss or give you an edge in the job market can give your career the kickstart you've been looking for. Don't play it safe. You never want to think, *What if?*

"Be focused. Be determined. Be hopeful. Be empowered. Empower yourselves with a good education, then get out there and use that education to build a country worthy of your boundless promise."
—MICHELLE OBAMA

Similarly, if you are even thinking about starting your own business, going back to school to get the proper training can be the most powerful tool you can have. There are so many moving parts to running your own company and it can be very overwhelming. If you don't know what you're doing, your business will suffer. When Taylor and I were starting our company, we took a course with an organization called Launch that provides training to small business owners, and they helped us learn how to build TTM the right way.

If at First You Don't Succeed...

Nobody enjoys failure, but the simple truth is that the road to success is often paved with failure. Failure does not come from trying, it comes from never having tried in the first place. Even Thomas Edison failed thousands of times before he invented the light bulb.

> *"I've missed more than 9,000 shots in my career. I've lost almost 300 games. 26 times, I've been trusted to take the game winning shot and missed. I've failed over and over and over again in my life. And that is why I succeed."*
>
> –MICHAEL JORDAN

If you do go out on a limb and try something new in your career, even if it doesn't work out the way you hoped, that is not a failure. Learn from your mistakes. Examine what you could have done differently, so that the next step you take will be the one that leads you to success.

Know Your Destination

Whether you are running your own business or working your way up the corporate ladder, always have a sense of your goals. Where do you want to be a year from now or ten years from now? If you don't at least have a sense of where you are going, in all likelihood, you won't get anywhere at all. You might not always know *how* to get there, but you should at least have a clear idea of the direction you're heading.

Chapter 5

WHAT TO EXPECT... THAT YOU WEREN'T EXPECTING

Warning: This chapter contains information that—unless you are a mother, an expectant mother, or even just thinking of becoming a mother one day—may be more than you ever wanted to know about what happens to the female body before, during, and after labor. If you are none of the above, I encourage you to skip ahead to the next chapter before it is too late!

I realized recently that I have arrived at a time in my life when it seems like every few months I receive a "We're having a baby!" announcement from one of my friends. As a "veteran" mother of three, I am often asked to share information that I found to be helpful during my own experiences with pregnancy, labor, and delivery. So, here goes...

Whether you are getting advice from other moms or reading every book you can get your hands on to prepare for your baby, more often than not what you will find is that a lot of the information out there is mainly focused on your developing fetus, pregnancy cravings, morning sickness, breast feeding tips, and baby products. But there are things that are going to happen to your body during and after pregnancy that most new mothers have no clue to ask about, much less to expect. When I was pregnant with Bentley, I was all of sixteen. Didn't you know that sixteen-year-old girls

> *"I feel like when I arrive at the hospital, I want a glass of whiskey, I want the epidural in my back, and I want to get hit in the face with a baseball bat."*
> –KRISTEN BELL

know absolutely everything there is to know about everything? So, of course, I assumed I knew it all and had no reason to suspect that pregnancy and labor (at any age) would be anything but wondrous, beautiful, and clean. Boy, was I wrong—especially about the clean part.

Wait, you mean labor isn't just sucking on ice chips, breathing through contractions, and having your partner massage your feet? Fortunately for me, my mother was there to quickly put an end to this fantasy and bring me back down somewhere closer to reality. After enlightening me on all of the joys and trials of pregnancy, she then filled me in on some messy truths about what happens during and after labor that nobody (much less an overconfident, hormonally supersized teenager) is ever prepared to hear. And to be honest, even after being told what to expect, I was still unprepared for what was about to happen to my body.

LIFE LESSONS

Many women experience **nausea** and **vomiting** during the birthing process. Others may experience **diarrhea** or **flatulence** before or during labor. While pushing, a woman may lose control of her bladder or bowels.

Source: unitypoint.org

After nine months of pregnancy and all the bizarre and wonderful changes that your body goes through, you might imagine that nothing that comes after labor could surprise you. You would be wrong. Believe it or not, nothing during pregnancy can prepare you for the things that your body does after you deliver the baby. So here is everything soon-to-be moms need—but don't necessarily want—to know about labor and beyond.

Hello Baby! Goodbye Modesty!

I was always somewhat shy when it came to things like going to the bathroom or changing clothes in front of my girlfriends, but after having my hoo-ha in plain view for a room full of people to see during labor, nurses helping me get cleaned up after I had given birth, and being examined *down there* countless times before I left the hospital... I realized that as I was welcoming my brand new baby boy into the world, I was also waving goodbye to that part of me that gave a damn about modesty. My advice: Get Over It. There's no one in that room who hasn't seen it all before, and the reality is everyone is so focused on the baby that has recently come out of you that they are not thinking about your vagina at all.

LIFE LESSONS

The birthing process isn't quite over once the baby is born. A woman must still **deliver the placenta** if she gave birth vaginally. After a woman gives birth to her baby, she will continue to have **mild contractions**. The woman's healthcare provider may rub her stomach to encourage the uterus to **expel** the placenta, or the woman may have to push a few more times after giving birth.

Source: unitypoint.org

Wait... What Is That? Is That Normal?

After my beautiful Bentley made his way into the world, it seemed as though my vagina immediately became an emergency exit for everything else inside of me. After you have exhausted every ounce (and more) of your strength and energy pushing and laboring your child into the world, you might think your job is done. It isn't. I couldn't count on two hands (or perhaps more accurately, *hold* in two hands) all the things the doctor pulled out of me during and after labor. Faced with no other option, I decided that since the doctor and nurses seemed to be fine with my hoo-ha throwing things at them, then I would have to be fine with it too.

If you're thinking to yourself, *Tell me what came out. What exactly was it?* Well, that's a damn good question. Here's what I know:

- **Placenta:** (Also known as *afterbirth.*) This miraculous organ, that connects your unborn baby to the wall of your uterus, does everything from provide nutrition and oxygen to baby, to regulate temperature, to remove waste from baby's blood. But once baby moves out, the placenta must go.

- **Mucus and Tissue:** From your uterus—mostly from the site where the placenta was attached to the uterine wall.

- **Blood:** Lots of it. Within the first ten minutes after delivery, it is natural to lose up to a pint of blood—and in some cases more.

It Will Have You in Stitches

An episiotomy is a procedure (there's no gentle way to say this) in which a small surgical cut is made into the *perineum* (that's the medical term for the area between your vagina and rectum) to extend the vaginal opening during delivery. After delivery, the doctor will stitch the episiotomy and other tears with dissolvable sutures.

Just thinking about it makes me shudder, but the fact is that about one in five women in the US will have an episiotomy during vaginal labor. The point of the episiotomy is to make delivery easier for mommy and baby. Years ago, episiotomies were believed to prevent tearing of the vagina and damage to the pelvic floor. However, recent studies have shown that vaginal tears cause less pain and bleeding than episiotomies and that pelvic floor damage is more likely to occur with an episiotomy than with a tear. Although there are cases where episiotomies cannot be avoided, if you are pregnant and have concerns I recommend talking to your OB/GYN in advance to discuss your options.

With Maverick, my delivery was a breeze because he was my third, but with Jayde and Bentley I tore and had to have a couple of stitches. In the hospital, they gave me Percocet but it made me nauseous and sleepy. If you have a similar reaction I recommend asking for 800 mg ibuprofen. It works well and (for me at least) there are fewer side effects.

LIFE LESSONS

According to the American College of Obstetricians and Gynecologists, between 1983 and 2000, the **episiotomy rate** in the US fell from about **70%** of all vaginal births to about **20%**.

Source: parents.com

Diapers for Two

Even after all of the *stuff* that left my body after delivery, it still came as a bit of a shock when I realized that my son wasn't going to be the only one wearing diapers. Bleeding will continue (like a heavy period) for about 3 to 10 days, and light bleeding and spotting can occur for up to 6 weeks after your child is born. Tampons—and sex, for that matter—are off limits for the first six weeks because they can introduce bacteria into your uterus. So stock up on heavy-duty pads—they will become your best friend

The Real Reason Your Boobs Exist

Don't think for a second that the only part of your body leaking will be your lower region. Milk, milk, and more milk. Even if you choose not to breastfeed, there will be a window (from a few days to a couple of weeks) before your milk dries up, so be sure to take advantage of what I like to call "bra diapers": the awkward and uncomfortable—yet absolutely essential—pads that you place inside your bra to prevent you from having to walk around in a milk-soaked shirt and smelling like cottage cheese.

> *"I'm busy milking all day long. I feel like I have probably lost a good 75 percent of my brain power.... I say it halved itself and it halved itself again. It's not just the sleep deprivation, it is the breastfeeding and I call it the 'lactose lobotomy.'"*
>
> —NAOMI WATTS

A word of caution: never assume that just because you stopped leaking for a moment, that you are safe to pop out for quick trip to the store without inserting your bra diapers...you will never make it. *Your* baby is not the only infant able to *activate your lactate*. Just when you think you're about to make it through the checkout line without a leak, some baby two aisles over will start crying, and *boom,* your boobs are on a mission.

Where Did My Stomach Go?

In the hours and days after your baby is born, you may find yourself asking, "Why do I still look like I'm six months pregnant?" Remember: over the course of the past nine months your uterus has been slowly expanding from the size of a grapefruit to the size of a watermelon. It can take up to six weeks for it to shrink back to its normal size, but I promise you that it will.

Be prepared for your belly to feel like a memory foam mattress when you touch it after giving birth. This lasted a while for me. At first, I couldn't comprehend why my stomach felt this way. Eventually, I decided that it was to provide a comfortable spot for my baby to sleep on. That seemed logical enough for me (and, to be honest, at that point I had learned not to ask questions that I didn't really want to know the answers to).

LIFE LESSONS

Each year in the United States, there are approximately **six million pregnancies**. This means that at any one time, about **4% of women** in the US are pregnant.

Source: Americanpregnancy.org

Don't Freak Out

The good news is that while most of this is happening you're either too busy, too in love with your baby, or too exhausted to actually sit around and dwell on all the weird things happening to your body.

Something to remember: it is normal for everyone to experience these things, and it doesn't last forever. Though it all seemed to be a bit insane while I was going through it, I understood that it was all a part of the miracle that is bringing life into the world and I am still amazed at what my body is capable of.

If you are an expecting mom for the first time this was probably a lot of information to take in and may even be hard to accept...but when it was my time to face these facts, I was thankful that my mom had attempted to prepare me for what no book ever could.

Chapter 6

MOTHER

[muhth-er] – noun
1. One person who does the work of twenty (for free).
2. The most underappreciated person on the planet.
(See also: 'hero,' 'badass,' **'saint'***)*

Whether you have one child, ten, or none at all, we've all been guilty of it at one time or another: Mom shaming. If you have ever recoiled at the sight of a mother in the supermarket picking up her crying child's dropped binky and "cleaning" it in her own mouth, shot an impatient look at a frazzled mom in a restaurant whose toddler just will not sit quietly and behave, or felt superior listening to a mommy friend's bedtime struggles because *you* would *never* have let *your* baby sleep in your bed that long, you are passing judgment when you should be sending vibes of respect and solidarity!

Being a young mother, I have been experiencing mom shaming pretty much since the day Bentley was born; and the fact that I am on television means that everything I do is open to public scrutiny. I have learned not to let it get me down, but it never ceases to amaze me how quick

Bonnie all snuggled up with Maverick for their midmorning nap.

people are to pass judgment. I'll give you an example. Not so long ago Taylor posted a photo on Instagram that opened me up to all kinds of criticism. In the photo, I'm lying on the couch, holding my daughter, Jayde, who was about three months old at the time. She was swaddled in her blanket and sleeping, well, like a baby. We were doing our fantasy football draft and I was holding a bottle of beer. Taylor innocently posted the photo with the tag, #draftday.

The reaction that followed was intense. People accused me of being a horrible, negligent mother; of drinking too much; of putting my newborn in mortal danger. *It's one beer, folks.* I am an adult, over the legal drinking age, and just because I'm a mom that doesn't mean I can't enjoy a beer on a Sunday evening with my husband. I've also had similar reactions to pictures I've posted of my kids with our dogs (two boxers, Bonnie and Clyde, who definitely live up to their names). People will comment that they can't believe I would let my kids near such a vicious breed of dog. I don't know if they're confusing boxers with pit bulls, but either way they are passing judgment on a situation they know nothing about.

At 40 lbs., Bonnie is petite for a boxer. Clyde, on the other hand, weighs in at 105 lbs. pounds and is taller than me when he stands up on his hind legs. But he has no idea he's the bigger of the two, and when they lie on the couch together he just wraps himself around Bonnie and snuggles. We adopted both of them from a shelter that rescues abused boxers, and they are the gentlest, sweetest family dogs you could ever hope for. Jayde especially loves Bonnie and Clyde. Whenever she's in her highchair eating, she will take a bite of her food (*one for Jayde*) and then feed a piece to Bonnie *(one for Bonnie)*, and then feed a piece to Clyde (*one for Clyde*—and so on, you get the picture). If you know my dogs, you would know how ridiculous the idea of them attacking my children is. But that's the problem with passing judgment; it's usually based on ignorance and presumption rather than actual facts.

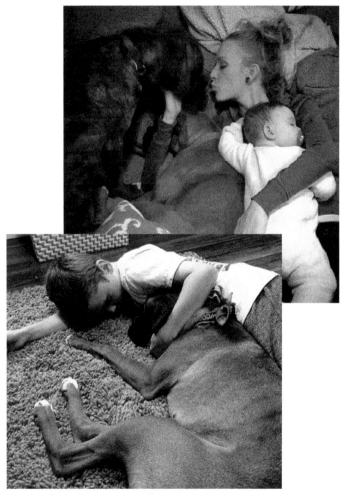

Top: Jayde and I napping with my fur babies, Bonnie and Clyde. *Bottom:* Bentley and Bonnie.

LIFE LESSONS

According to a survey of 227 moms conducted in October 2016 by the mobile app mom.life, **80% of moms** (that's 4 out of every 5 moms) have been victims of mom shaming:

- 67% of those who had been shamed were shamed **by other moms**;
- 64% of those who had been shamed were shamed for their **feeding choice**;
- 4 in 10 moms have been shamed online, and 1 in 3 moms have been shamed **via phone or text**;
- But less than 0.5 percent of moms changed their behaviors because of mom shaming.

Source: Huffingtonpost.com

Social media only magnifies the problem. I hear stories all the time from friends who post happy pics of a day out with their kids only to find themselves on the receiving end of angry mom shaming comments. A friend of mine, who is in the public eye because her husband is a professional athlete, posted a pic of her son watching the popcorn in the microwave. She got crazy comments that she was going to fry her son's brain from standing too close to the microwave. Another friend of mine posted a pic of her son wearing a T-shirt with the graphic "ALL boy" and people wrote to her that the shirt was sexist. It's not clear if they felt he should be wearing a T shirt that said "ALL girl," but what is clear is that opinions are like assholes, everyone's got one and most of them are full of shit.

> *"Why do people feel they have the right to criticize a parent about their own children without having any facts?... Those who criticize, think twice about what you say about other people's children because actually you have no right to criticize me as a parent."*
>
> —David Beckham

To all those who pass judgment on other moms I say, mind your own eff'ing beeswax!! Newsflash: *Mothers Are Human Beings*. We are flawed, hard-working, well-intentioned, exhausted individuals; we do our best, we make mistakes, but above all we love our children. While obviously I don't condone excessive drinking, having a beer—or even smoking the occasional cigarette—does not warrant a call to Child Services, and it does *not* make you a bad mother.

Momma Don't Preach

For the longest time I was the only one among my friends who had a child, and because I was the only mom around I thought it was my job to mother everyone around me. But there's a fine line between offering friendly advice and sticking your nose where it doesn't belong. I have often been guilty of thinking *my* way is the *right* way, and then enthusiastically spreading my gospel to my friends.

When Bentley was a baby I didn't have mommy friends, so when my good friend Katie and I got pregnant at the same time I was thrilled. It wasn't planned, but our daughters, Jayde and Ava, were born five days apart. Without really realizing why, I immediately found myself trying to correct Katie if I felt she was doing something the "wrong" way. I offered all kinds of advice, even though she never asked for it. I guess I had decided that it was my job to take over and offer her all of the wisdom of my experience.

I remember the moment I realized my good intentions had become overbearing. It happened to be about Ava sleeping in the bed with her. Probably after the fifth time over the course of a year that I had advised her to transition Ava to a crib, it finally dawned on me I wasn't getting much of a response from Katie. She was politely listening, but clearly she wasn't taking my advice. I took a step back and realized I was being kind of obnoxious. She probably didn't give a damn what I had to say. I said to myself, *You've told her enough times now that if she was going to take your advice, she would have done it already.* Although you may think you are helping, sometimes your good intentions can cross the line. Know when it's time to keep your opinions to yourself

It's All in The Delivery

If you have real advice, by all means give it...but don't judge. I once posted a pic of Jayde in her car seat and someone (who actually had some manners) posted a respectfully worded comment that we had her strapped in wrong. I looked it up and, sure enough, she was right. In this case, I was grateful someone pointed out my mistake, and because she had approached me in a way that wasn't aggressive or judgmental, I was able to actually "hear" what she was saying.

There are times when someone has said to me something like, "I noticed you were [enter mommy mistake/struggle here]. I don't know if you've tried [enter mommy solution here], but it really worked for me." If a person approaches me this way, especially if he or she isn't a close friend or a part of my family, I'm much more likely to listen to what they have to say than to feel defensive. If you present your advice with that kind of here's-a-different-way-to-go-about-it tone that says you can take-my-advice-or-leave-it, how you come across becomes more about sharing than preaching. If your intentions are good and your tone respectful, your advice will most likely be well received. If not, that person does not want your advice and you're better off keeping your opinions to yourself.

Ain't Too Proud... to Ask for Help

I've always said it doesn't matter if your sixteen or sixty, nothing can prepare you at all for motherhood. The difference for me is that I was a teenager when my first son was born so I was even more stubborn than I am now.

In a way, I had to be because at the time I felt that was the only way for me to make it. So, in the beginning, I kind of ignored everyone and did what I felt was best for me and Bentley.

Now I am much more willing to ask for help or advice than I was at sixteen. Bentley was an easy baby, Jayde too. Maverick, my third, had more issues with sleeping and was diagnosed with silent reflux, which can easily be misinterpreted as fussiness because there are no visible symptoms other than inconsolable crying. His pediatrician prescribed him medicine to reduce stomach acidity and help relieve the pain, but every time we gave it to him he would push it out with his tongue or he would get so upset that he would throw the medicine right back up.

It was frustrating and upsetting watching my baby get so worked up, but then a mom friend shared a genius tip with me. If you gently squeeze your baby's cheeks together, it makes their mouth open to an O shape and then you squeeze the medicine into his or her mouth with a dropper. It's going to piss your baby off, but he/she won't be able stick out his/her tongue. Your baby's gag reflex will kick in and he/she will swallow the medicine. There's a world of experienced mothers out there, so don't be afraid to ask for help when you need it.

MOMMY HACKS

- Did you know that baby **onesies that have snaps on the shoulder** are meant to be put on feet first and then pulled up? Then when you take it off, you pull it back down towards their feet. If you've ever had to change a wriggling cranky baby, with an **explosive diaper** where the poop has traveled up his/her back, this will come in handy because as you roll the onesie down **all the poop gets rolled up** with it. No mess, minimal fuss!

- This may be a Southern mom redneck thing, but if your child is **coughing** or something goes down the wrong pipe, **raise his/her arm** and hold it up in the air. It will open up their windpipe and help them breath. It **works like a charm**, every time. To this day when Bentley starts coughing, I don't have to say a thing; he just automatically sticks his arm in the air.

- In the early stages of pregnancy, you can put off wearing maternity clothes for a bit by taking an **elastic hair tie**, wrapping it around the button of your favorite jeans, pulling it through the hole and then **looping it around** the button again. This little trick will save you money on maternity clothes and give you a few extra weeks in your favorite **pre-pregnancy jeans**.

Let 'em Learn

We all parent differently. One person's Helicopter Parenting is another's Attachment Parenting. I happen to be a big believer in giving your children enough space to learn for themselves. Recently, for example, Jayde was trying to climb over the couch and Taylor's mom said to me, "Should we stop her?" I said, "Let her go. If she falls, she'll learn." And, sure enough, she fell and busted her gum on the corner of the couch. Jayde cried, and she bled, but she survived...and she's never climbed over the back of the couch again.

Food for Thought

I don't do the whole organic thing and I don't make my kids' baby food—there's plenty of healthy, affordable, and flavorful options available in supermarkets these days. I don't know enough about the benefits of organic over non-organic baby food to argue one way or the other, but what I do know is that the most important thing is for your children to develop a healthy attitude to food and nutrition early on. If you encourage your kids to try different foods, to moderate their intake of refined sugars, and if you make meals into fun, family time then you will be laying the foundation for a lifetime of healthy eating habits.

Recipe for a mother's love
    By: Chef Bentley

    One pinch of kisses
    three cups of love
    One teaspoon of smiles
    One cup of hugs

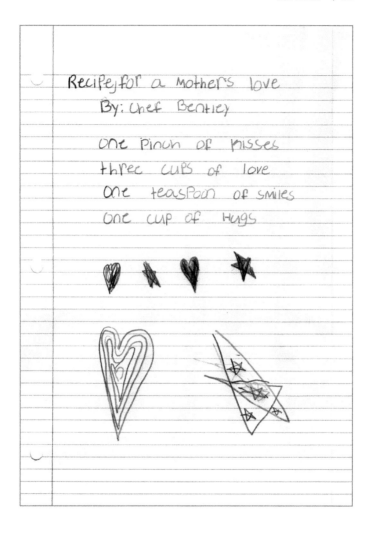

Stretching: The Truth

This may be the single most important tip I can give any expectant mother: as soon as you find out you're pregnant, *slather yourself in cocoa butter*. They day I told my mother I was pregnant with Bentley, she went out to Walmart and bought me a giant tub of cocoa butter. She said, "If you use this every single day of your pregnancy, you won't get stretch marks."

It works. But you have to be vigilant, and not just with your stomach. Throughout your pregnancy, your baby is gradually growing and so are you. No matter your skin size or body type, keeping your skin supple during pregnancy will prevent dreaded stretch marks. During all three of my pregnancies, I kept a gallon tub under my sink, another in my car, another in my desk at work. I always give every single one of my girlfriends a care package of cocoa butter early in their pregnancies. Not one of them has stretch marks.

"I love our daughters more than anything in the world—more than life itself. And while that may not be the first thing that some folks want to hear from an Ivy-League-educated lawyer, it is truly who I am. So for me, being Mom-in-Chief is, and always will be, job number one."

–Michelle Obama

To Work or to Stay-at-Home

I want to be absolutely clear: Being at home with your children is a full-time job. If you choose to follow that path, it can be a joyous one. If you are truly fulfilled being home with your children, enriching their lives with your love and laughter, then that is your true path. You won't miss a single second of your children's most precious moments.

> "NBC has me under contract. The baby and I have only a verbal agreement."
> –TINA FEY

But, it is also valid to have the need to exist beyond your children; whether that need is borne of financial necessity, creative drive, or intellectual enrichment. Again, for some those needs are fulfilled by being home with your children, but for others pursuing an education or a career will actually make you a better mother. I couldn't be home with my kids full time. I need an outlet outside the home. That doesn't mean I love my children any less. It just means that I recognize my limitations and that I am striving to be the best person I can be—*for* my children. It's important to have your own interests and passions. Work, for me, is an escape from the kids. And then home is an escape from work. For me, it's a good balance.

The Great Bed Debate

I'm all for everyone doing what works for them when it comes to sleeping with your baby. All of my babies slept in the bed with me until they were eight weeks old. (I know, I know. I'll probably get angry tweets from the you're-going-to-smother-your-baby lobby, but I believe it promotes bonding—and, honestly, it's the only way you'll get any sleep those first few weeks.) After that, be warned: the longer you let baby sleep in your bed, the harder it's going to be to get baby out of your bed. That's all I'm going to say about that.

Sibling Rivalry

There's nothing quite so intense as the rush of pure, unadulterated love you experience the first time you look into the depthless eyes that are the window to your first child's newborn soul. So it's only natural that when you become pregnant with your second child, you might freak out that you won't be capable of loving your new baby as much, or that loving the second might somehow take something away from the first. Not true. That is the miracle of a mother's love: it is infinite. There is as much love in your heart for the first as there is for the second.

When you get to the third... that's when things get intense. Oh, yeah, there's plenty of love to go around. There's just not enough arms, or pairs of eyes, or hours of

My little blended family.

sleep in the day. While I was pregnant with Jayde, Taylor and I had talked about the possibility of adopting a third much (much!) further down the road. We never planned on my getting pregnant again so soon after she was born. Maverick was totally unexpected. When I found out I was pregnant, Jayde was still a baby. I was working full time, starting a new clothing line with Taylor, and we had just started filming for a new season of *Teen Mom*. Bentley was just getting settled in school and starting to play sports. All I could think was, *How am I going to handle all of this? There's not going to be enough of me to go around.* It took me a couple of months to wrap my mind around the change. It helped that Taylor and Bentley were very excited about the baby, but if truth be told I was terrified.

I still remember my dad's reassuring words when I told him that I was pregnant with Maverick and confided to him that I questioned my capacity to handle three children, two of them born a year and a day apart. He said to me, "It's normal for you to feel that way. Just remember that if God didn't want you to have these babies, he wouldn't have given them to you." Everything happens for a reason. My children were given to me because I was strong enough to care for them...I just didn't know it yet.

> *"Any woman who understands the problems of running a home will be nearer to understanding the problems of running a country."*
> –Margaret Thatcher

Family Circus

If you are blessed with two children who were born a year apart, the biggest piece of advice I can give you: Don't lose your mind, or your sense of humor. There is no question that at times it will be chaos. Having two children under the age of two is not for the faint of heart. You will be sleep deprived. You will be irritable. You will be covered in bodily fluids. But your home will be full of love, laughter and joy—and poopy diapers.

Taylor and I, we make a very good team. In some households, things are still very traditional as far as the dad working and the mom handling everything in the house. Even though some aspects of our marriage are

Taylor and I are equal partners.

traditional, we both work and we are both responsible for cleaning the house, doing laundry, and generally taking care of the kids. It's a 50–50 split.

The biggest thing is just acceptance. We have three kids. We are tired. We are stressed out. But we are blessed. Triply blessed. There are so many people out there who want children, but can't have them. You can dwell on the things that make it stressful, or you can have fun in your crazy circus of a family.

Chapter 7

#AINT #NOBODY #GOT #TIME #FOR #THAT

This chapter is dedicated to those who have a special way of making me silently mouth, "What the hell?" after reading something you've posted on social media. I pray you come across this chapter and take the hint. (Please don't be offended. I'm simply trying to help—hell, you may even thank me later!)

Let's face it; there is no escaping social media. We are at the dawn of a new millennium, and social media has become as fundamental to the laws of the universe as gravity. It's safe to say that 99% of the people I know personally currently use one form of social media or another. A few years back even my grandfather, who agitatedly used to ask my grandmother why she was always on "that MyFace bullshit," broke down and made a page of his own—although it was on Facebook, not MyFace (I'm fairly certain MyFace isn't a thing, but you never know with social media—or my grandfather for that matter.) Come to think of it...if my grandparents are active on Facebook, then

that 1% of people I know personally who are *not* currently using
social media is made up entirely
of children under the age of two.
Shit, actually, even some of them
have their own pages.

> *"With great power comes
> great responsibility."*
> –"Uncle Ben" Parker

There are multiple platforms from which to choose,
each with millions of users around the world. With just
a few swipes of the finger, you might use Facebook to
connect with old friends, create a shared album of photos
on Instagram, update your career skills and network on
LinkedIn, use Twitter to stay on top of trending topics,
and "wink" at a couple of cuties on Match.com—all before
you've even finished your morning cup of coffee. Social
media is how we get involved and stay connected. In
today's world, if you are not on social media you may as
well not exist.

Social media has its perks, and I firmly believe people
should use it to full advantage. *But...* according to the
laws of the universe, a positive force is inevitably accom-
panied by its equally powerful negative counterpart. I'm
not talking about the social media platforms themselves;
I'm referring to some of the creatures that populate them.
Trolls. Catfish. Cyberbullies. Insecure and self-serving
monsters, who lurk in the shadows and feed on vanity,
controversy, and attention.

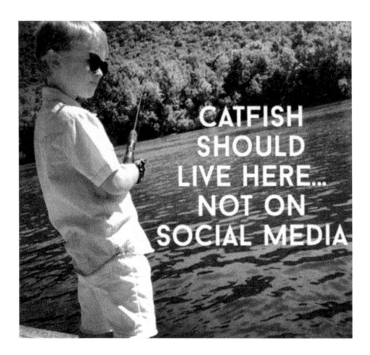

If you're like me, you don't remember exactly the point at which social media completely infiltrated your life. You just woke up one day and realized that your every waking moment (from your Instagram of that perfect leaf on your morning latte, to the pin of your dream jeans, or your after-work #happyhour group selfie) is filtered through one of dozens of apps on your phone. Unfortunately, there is no guidebook for navigating the complicated and

> *"Arguing with anonymous strangers on the Internet is a sucker's game because they almost always turn out to be—or to be indistinguishable from—self-righteous sixteen-year-olds possessing infinite amounts of free time."*
>
> –NEAL STEPHENSON, AUTHOR *CRYPTONOMICON*

often treacherous terrain of social media; the technology is so new that for the most part we are in uncharted territory. However, there are some basic social media dos and don'ts, which if we all followed would vastly improve our virtual lives.

At least once a day, I find myself wanting to ask people I encounter on social media, "Is this really the image you want to project to the world?" (There are even a few people I'd like to mention here by name, but *ain't nobody got time for that*.)

LIFE LESSONS

More than **one-out-of-seven** people in the world use **Facebook**, and people post well over **200 billion tweets** per year.

Source: fastcompany.com

REASONS WE ALL NEED A "DISLIKE" BUTTON

- 👎 People who **tweet bash their own team** when they're down 23 to 7 in the fourth quarter, but are the first to jump up and down when they execute a come from behind win.
- 👎 **New Year's resolutions.** (You are exactly the same person today that you were a year ago, and just like last year that new diet or workout routine isn't going to see the end of January.)
- 👎 People who **retweet** constantly, but never have anything original to say.
- 👎 *Anyone* who **live tweets** during an awards show.
- 👎 Incoherent, borderline-psycho, **political rants**.
- 👎 **Celebrity death** tweets. Save your tears for people you actually know.
- 👎 **Slacktivism**—posting a video of the #icebucketchallenge does not make you a philanthropist.
- 👎 **Autocorrect apathy.** Please, please, proofread before posting.
- 👎 There's never any need for **ALL CAPS!!!!**

Likes Won't Make Your Dirty Laundry Any Cleaner

Have you ever thought about why people refer to information of a particularly personal and private nature as *dirty laundry*? Well, simply because that is exactly what it is; it looks and smells like shit, it's usually embarrassing, and as far as I know not a soul in the world enjoys being exposed to it. I don't even like thinking about my own dirty laundry, so what in the hell makes you think that I would want to be exposed to yours?

"Don't worry laundry, nobody wants to do me either."

—Unknown

Is all the oversharing really necessary? Nobody wants to know that you sat too long on the tanning bed and fried your ass, nor do we need to hear every single detail of your on-again, off-again relationship. When you use social media to air your dirty laundry or as a perch from which to tweet your TMI with abandon, it makes me want to clothesline *you*.

GET YOUR DIRT OFF MY FACE

Line Leaders Can't Exist if No One Is Standing Behind Them

America is the land of the free and the home of the brave. Isn't it beautiful that we are free to choose our own beliefs and to express our opinions? I welcome an interesting and respectful debate. I respect other people's educated positions on issues involving our country's leaders, even when they differ from mine. I can respect people who share their political opinions on social media, if they choose to do so. *But*, I do not condone people who use social media to publicly disrespect the leaders of our country. Y'all do realize that anyone in the entire world can see what you share on social media, right? You can *and* should be able to express yourself without coming across like a complete dipshit. In my opinion, when people publicly bash our leaders on global social media platforms, it makes our country look weak. I find it quite embarrassing. Keep in mind: there is no line without a leader, no leader without a line.

Your Monthly Gym Membership Should Look Like This...

Workout Fee. *$5*
Wi-Fi Fee *$20*

I'm embarrassed to admit that I know exactly which day of the week "Leg Day" is for a few people that I follow on social media. I involuntarily gained this knowledge from (over)exposure to posts about their workouts every-single-damn-day-five-days-a-damn-week. I'm happy for all of you who, unlike me, actually enjoy going to the gym. But, quite frankly, I don't give a shit if you're fit. And most of the time, when I see your daily "#getfit #healthylife #sweat" post, in my head I'm thinking: *Man, if you spent your time actually working out instead*

THE ARTICLE YOU SHARED WAS FAKE

BUT THAT'S NONE OF MY BUSINESS

of posting that gym selfie, we would be in a win-win situation: you would be a lot more fit, and I would avoid damaging my eye muscles from involuntarily rolling them every time I'm exposed to a post of your workout routine. Basically, if your smartphone automatically connects to your gym's Wi-Fi network, you're probably posting from the gym too much.

Facebook Is Not CNN

Bloggers are not reporters. They are people with opinions. There's a place for this in national newspapers as well; it's called an editorial. The difference between a legitimate piece of reporting and an opinion piece is that the former is an unbiased assessment of facts and the latter is one individual's perspective. With legitimate news outlets, it is clear which you are reading; with social media that line is not just blurry, it has a BAC of 0.25.

The problem with this shift in how we get our information is that most people assume that if it's on social media then it must be fact. According to a Pew Research Center poll, 35% of American voters between the ages of 18 and 20 reported social media as their main source of information during the 2016 election. And we all know where that got us. All I can say is educate yourself. There's a lot of good, useful information on the Internet, but there's also hella people out there who have their own agenda—and it's rarely what's in *your* best interests.

LIFE LESSONS

According to a 2016 survey by the **Pew Research Center**, a majority of US adults (62%) get **news on social media**, and 18% do so often.

- Two-thirds of **Facebook** users (66%) get news on the site.
- Nearly six-in-ten **Twitter** users (59%) get news on Twitter.
- Seven-in-ten **Reddit** users (70%) get news on that platform.
- On **Tumblr**, the figure sits at 31%.

Source: journalism.org

Know What You're Sharing

Most people want to be perceived by others as informed and articulate. To that end: Stop sharing articles, news, and links before you've actually read the damn things yourself. Remember that your social media presence is a direct reflection of who you are in the real world. More than likely, you wouldn't speak in person on a subject if you didn't have some prior knowledge on which to base your opinion. Or would you?

Too often I see people sharing articles or stories that they clearly didn't read prior to sharing them. From my experience of being in the public eye, I'll let you in on a little secret: the media has to grab your attention, and believe me they will do *anything* to get it. In this world of attention-deficit surfing, the media better than anyone know that if they don't grab you with catchy and alarming titles like "New Weight Loss Method 'Shrinks' Fat Cells Overnight" it's likely they will never get your attention. But beware: titles can be very misleading, and sometimes even false. Please study before you share.

Freedom from Your Phone

My New Year's resolution was to break free from the shackles of my smartphone—I know I've done a good job with it because my friends keep asking where I've been

> *"The Internet is becoming the town square for the global village of tomorrow."*
>
> —BILL GATES, FOUNDER OF MICROSOFT

and why I'm not answering my texts. Put your phone down. Be in the moment.

Our attachment to our devices has become so "normal" that I've literally been out with someone who tweeted me while we were sitting across from one another at a restaurant. I was like, *Dude, I'm sitting right across from you. You could have leaned over and just told me that in 140 characters or less.* If you find yourself watching concerts through the camera on your phone and keeping a spare charger in your car (and your purse, and your desk, and your boyfriend's apartment), then it's time to disconnect.

Check Please!

My close friends and I have a thing where, when we go out as a group, we all place our phones in the middle of the table and you cannot touch it until the meal is over. If it rings someone else can answer, but if it's not an emergency (if your kids aren't vomiting, or your house isn't on fire) you can't take the call. The penalty for picking up your phone before the end of the meal, is that you have to pay for everyone else at the table. Since we started this rule, not one of us has picked up her phone before the check came.

Chapter 8

LIKE THE ONE YOU'RE WITH

"I used to ask my dad, 'How did you and Mom stay married all this time?' and he'd say, 'Two things. Number 1: You gotta have the same dreams... [Number 2:] We never wanted to get divorced at the same time.'"

–GWYNETH PALTROW

From the time we are old enough to understand what it means when Prince Charming kisses awaken Sleeping Beauty from her enchanted slumber, we are conditioned to believe that love is the most powerful force in the world. But, honestly, "like" is what keeps a relationship alive. Once the fireworks have fizzled out, something more solid (and less flammable) has to take their place. Happily Ever After is a marathon, not a sprint.

For most of my life I would walk into relationships already convinced that it wasn't going to work; at some point there's going to be a catch and when something bad happens I'm gonna run. I wouldn't allow myself to be vulnerable. My shields were up, so I couldn't really be present in any of my relationships. The thing is, if you go looking for problems, you'll usually find them.

It wasn't until Taylor and I got serious that I finally began to understand that the *problem* wasn't necessarily our *problems*. He seemed so perfect. I kept asking myself, *When is something bad going to happen? When is the fatal flaw in our relationship going to reveal itself?* Eventually I realized, I could either walk away or give this great guy a chance. That's when I let my guard down. We all come with baggage, hell I know I do, but at the end of the day, if you enjoy one another's company you can take on anything life throws at you.

I finally found my soulmate.

LIFE LESSONS

Your **soulmate** is out there somewhere:

- According to the US Census Bureau, there are **95.9 million unmarried** people in the US, of which 47% are men and 53% are women.
- Psychologists at the University of Pennsylvania studied data from more than 10,000 speed daters and found that most people make a decision regarding a person's **attraction within three seconds of meeting**.
- Studies show that schools, colleges, coffee shops, and malls are all excellent **places to flirt** because people are more open to meeting others in these places. Poor locations are restaurants and movie theaters.
- 20 to 40 million Americans have used **online dating services**. Nearly 50% of online daters are aged 18–34, and 24% are 35–44.

Source: Randomhistory.com

Easy as 1, 2, 3

I believe we fall in love three times. The first love is magical, but most of the time you're too young or too inexperienced and over time the feelings fade away. It's hard to get over and even when you do, you feel like you'll never have that feeling again. Which is true.

Then you find your second person. There's butterflies and real feelings, but you don't really work together. You think this is the person you're supposed to be with, so you try to make them different or into what you need them to be.

Your third love is the person you never saw coming. You're so used to what wrong feels like that you don't recognize when it's right. It's a long process, but then you finally realize *this* is my person.

Every Relationship Needs a Little TLC*

- **Trust** is a critical component of any partnership. You need to be the healthiest you for your relationship. When trust is broken, you begin to question not just your partner but yourself, who *you* are. It turns into you questioning what you've done wrong and it immediately shuts you down.

- **Love making** is very important to a relationship. Most women need to *feel* intimate to be close, but most men need to *be* intimate to be close. Physical intimacy is how we express love without words and stay connected to one another.

- **Communication** is a two-way street. Sometimes it's best to not be the first one to talk. You have to remember that your significant other has needs and feelings, too. You also have to accept that you are not perfect and listen to how you are making your partner feel.

----

* There are no shortcuts here. You can't skip trust, and go straight to love making. You need all three components for a healthy relationship. Without trust and communication, you cannot have true physical intimacy.

> *"A relationship without trust is like a phone with no service. And what do you do with a phone with no service? You play games."*
>
> –DRAKE

Stop Using Sex as a Weapon

One common relationship mistake that I hear about over and over again is that when couples get into an argument, one of them (usually the woman) will withhold sex as a form of punishment. I can't stress enough how bad this is for your relationship. Once you begin to use physical intimacy as a form of leverage, it takes the passion away and sex becomes more of a transaction than an expression of love.

Time Together

It is absolutely essential to have alone time with your partner; time when your parents aren't around, your kids aren't around, your dogs aren't even around. I know, easier said than done. It helps to find a shared hobby or interest.

Taylor and I had always talked about golfing together, but we never seemed to find the time. With Maverick waking up four times a night, I would take the night shift and Taylor would get the kids up and ready for school and day care. We were like ships in the night. Then randomly one day, he came home and surprised me with a set of women's golf clubs he had found on Craigslist.

Now, every other week, no matter what else is going on in our lives, we'll clear our schedules to spend the day playing golf together. We're both competitive so, of course, we want to win, but it's more about taking the time to just have fun together with no kids and no distractions.

Theory of Evolution

Life is about growth. The person you are today will likely be very different from the person you will become five, ten, or twenty years from now. Change and growth are good for a relationship; the trick is to stay in tune with one another as you evolve.

Pay attention, ask questions, be attentive. With our busy schedules, we often end up living parallel lives, but when that happens you aren't evolving together and you just might wake up one day to find that you are in a relationship with a total stranger.

Be Spontaneous

One of Taylor's and my favorite songs is a duet by Kenny Chesney and Pink called "Setting the World on Fire." It's a romantic love song about those magical moments you have as a couple when you feel like the only two people in the world. Whenever it comes up in our playlist, no matter where we are, we crank it up and sing along with Pink and Chesney at the top of our voices.

"We were shoutin' out the window, like they could hear us at the pier.
Said 'Do you think we'll live forever?' as we killed another beer, and you wrote 'I love you' in lipstick on the mirror."

The more we listened to the song, the more meaningful it became for us. Then one day, I got the idea to dig up some red lipstick that I had used for Halloween and write, "I Love You," to Taylor on the bathroom mirror. I was a little worried he might think it was cheesy, but he totally got it. It was like a little secret between just the two of us.

Let's Get Physical

Sex isn't the only way to keep the physical chemistry in a relationship fresh and alive. Remember when you were in middle school and you got into a snowball fight with the boy you had a crush on, or your first slow dance with a cute boy? It was thrilling because you could feel the attraction, but it was still innocent and playful.

Taylor and I will have wrestling matches around the house or hold hands when we're in the car. Just because you are in a serious relationship, doesn't mean you shouldn't have fun and be playful. Flirtatious gestures of physical affection will keep your relationship young and exciting.

Relationship Karma

When it comes to relationships, the energy you give off creates a ripple effect that will determine not only the kind of person you are drawn to, but also how your partner responds to you. If you are closed off and guarded, that energy can manifest in any number of negative ways. You might find yourself repeating a pattern of falling into relationships with partners who are emotionally unavailable or pushing a healthy partner away for fear of becoming vulnerable. If you are needy and insecure, your energy might attract someone who is overbearing and controlling. But if you are open and responsive, that energy will feed your relationship with positivity.

Which One Are You?

If you identify with any of the following types, you've taken the first step toward breaking out of potentially negative relationship cycles. We've all been one or more of these types in a relationship, but if you fail to recognize these characteristics within yourself or your partner you will be doomed to repeat the same mistakes in one relationship after another.

The Fixer thinks they can change the person they're with. They tend to think the other person is the one with the problem, when really they need to look inward for the source of their unhappiness. (I am for sure a Fixer.)

The Victim is incapable of taking responsibility for their actions. When they've done something wrong, they blame their partner. They are not responsible for their actions because they were pushed to do it.

The Martyr feeds off dysfunction. They will always find themselves in unhealthy relationships because in their mind negative attention is better than no attention.

The Dictator always needs to be in control. This doesn't allow the partner to occupy any space in the relationship or to grow as an individual.

The Follower always takes on the interests and opinions of their partner, but in the process, loses touch with their own identity.

The Dependent would rather be in a toxic relationship than be alone.

You Knew it Was a Snake...

Here's a hard relationship truth: the kind of person you are attracted to is the kind of person you will end up in a relationship with. If you are drawn to a type of person who is emotionally available, monogamous, and loyal, it follows that those are the qualities that person will bring to the relationship. However, if you like bad boys, guess what? He's gonna be a bad boy in the relationship too. You knew it was a snake when you picked it up, so can you really be surprised when it bites you?

My most painful breakup was one where, because I had so much invested in the relationship, I convinced myself that I needed to make it work and ignored a lot of red flags. It was my second love, and my most toxic relationship. When it finally ended it was painful, but I also felt a sense of relief that the relationship was over. I realized that so much had happened in my life since I was sixteen, and I had never really taken the time to process any of it. I needed to figure out *me*.

Being in a healthy relationship means being honest with yourself about who you are and who you are with. More often than not when major issues come to a head in a relationship, they were there all along—we just chose to ignore them. Never sacrifice your own happiness to make it work with someone who doesn't respect you or isn't 100% committed to the relationship.

Unfortunately, it can be so easy to turn a blind eye to the obvious. You love someone and you want to make it work, so you ignore fundamental issues (like cheating or possessive behavior) and that's when you become a Fixer or a Martyr. You can spend years trying to salvage a doomed relationship, denying your own needs, or you can call a snake a snake, suck out the poison, and move on.

The Ex Files

When a relationship isn't working, we often stay in it too long out of some kind of misguided sense of loyalty, or

Take Me Back

I never thought you
would come back,
I never waited for you.
So please don't be upset
that I am unprepared.
I lost everything about me
when you left.
So please forgive me if that
is all I take with me,
When I run away this time.

worse, fear of being alone. Sometimes you grow apart, and that's okay as long as you are honest with yourself and your partner about how you are feeling. Sometimes it just makes more sense to cut your losses than to spend years frustratingly trying to force a square peg into a round hole.

With Ryan, it took a year of being disconnected, fighting, and living parallel lives before we finally split up. Because we were so young, we were focused on our own journeys. We stopped thinking about each other's needs, so the connection we had as a teen couple—and even during the pregnancy—was gone. We tried for a little while because we thought staying together was the right thing for Bentley (after all my parents have stayed together through all kinds of ups and downs since they were teenagers), but ultimately we realized that being happy and apart was far healthier for our son than being miserable and together.

No matter what, if you are not fully connected to your partner and fulfilled in your relationship, you will never truly be happy. This is not good for anyone—not for you, not for your partner, and definitely not for your children (if you have any). Though sometimes breaking up may seem harder than staying together, ending an unhappy, dysfunctional relationship is the right thing to do. In the long run, everyone involved will be happier.

For the Children

Whether a breakup is amicable or ugly, when there are children involved you can't just simply walk away and move on with your life. Having a child with someone means that no matter what, you will always be tied to each other. Therefore, it is absolutely essential that you

LIFE LESSONS

Many studies have shown that children whose divorced or separated parents have a cooperative relationship:

- **Feel secure.** Children who are confident in the love of both parents, adjust better to the separation and have better self-esteem.
- **Have consistency.** When you have similar rules, discipline, and rewards between households, children know what to expect, and what's expected of them.
- **Understand how to resolve conflict.** Children who observe their parents continuing to work together after separation learn how to effectively and peacefully solve problems themselves.
- **Have a healthy example to follow.** Healthy cooperation between parents, establishes healthy patterns that children will adopt in their own lives.

learn to set your issues aside and find a way to parent your children as separate but equal partners. Successful co-parenting means your kids will know that they are more important than whatever conflicts you and your partner may have, and that your love for them will not fade no matter what else changes in their lives.

In my situation, I have full custody of Bentley (in the state of Tennessee, if you have a child with someone that you are not or never were married to, custody is automatically given to the mother). However, as far as I am concerned Ryan is Bentley's father and that is more important than any issues he and I may have. No matter what is going on between us, or how angry I may have been at him in the past, at the end of the day it's not about me or how I feel anymore, it's about Bentley.

Let Go of the Past

Over the years, Ryan and I have definitely made mistakes, and a big one has been dredging up old fights. One of the most difficult aspects of co-parenting to master is not allowing the past to impact how you parent together in the present. It's almost impossible for two people to break up and not have lingering hurts and resentments, and it's easy for those feelings to flare up when sharing custody gets tricky.

Keep your issues with your ex away from your children. You may never completely get over your resentment or bitterness over certain issues, but you must remind yourself that they are *your* issues, not your child's. To successfully co-parent both parties have to learn to set the past aside and deal with one another as equal partners.

Children Are Not Leverage

The absolutely worst thing that one parent can do is to stand in the way of their child's relationship with the other parent. No matter what other problems we may have, or how angry I have felt, I would never take Ryan away from Bentley.

LIFE LESSONS

- More than **50% of first marriages** and 75% of second marriages **end in divorce**, as reported by Total Life Counseling Center.
- According to the Rebuilding Families website, more than **one million children** in the US experience the divorce of their biological parents each year.
- 65% of those children will end up in a **blended family** (a couple and their children from any previous relationships) due to the remarriage of one or both biological parents.
- According to The Bonded Family, almost **2,100 blended families** form in the United States every single day.
- *Business Innovators Magazine* predicts that the blended family will become the **predominant family structure** in the United States.

Source: lovetoknowy.com

Never use your kids as messengers; it puts them in the center of your conflict. The goal is to keep the children out of your relationship issues, so call or email your ex yourself. Be very careful never to say negative things about your ex in front of or to your children. Sometimes it can be a challenge not to vent your frustration, but doing so in their presence or within earshot will make them feel like they have to choose sides.

Communication and Respect

The two key ingredients to successful co-parenting are communication and respect. For a long time, Ryan and I just didn't talk because we didn't want to argue. We had been angry at one another for so long, we had forgotten that it was even possible to communicate without fighting. Eventually, we realized that not speaking was just as dysfunctional for Bentley as when we were arguing all the time. Now we are at a point where we can communicate with one another respectfully.

Whether you like it or not, the reality is that you are going to be parenting your kids until they are at least eighteen, so you might as well let go of all the bullshit and learn to work together. I always say we are "raising adults," so you have to act like the adults you want your children to become.

Chapter 9

CLIMB EVERY MOUNTAIN

When I was in 4th grade, my mom and dad took us on a family trip to Washington, DC. We went to all the monuments, the museums, and took a tour of the White House. I remember being totally in awe of the city—all the buildings, the history, and the people walking around everywhere—I had never seen anything like it. Just walking around the city, taking the bus and the metro, was a surreal experience. That was the first time I became aware that there was a whole world out there beyond my hometown, filled with strange and wonderful places. It was exciting, and a little bit scary at the same time.

After the first season of *16 & Pregnant* aired, MTV flew us to New York for the first reunion special. I had never been on a plane before, so that alone was a huge thrill. Even though I was much older and had seen enough movies and television shows to have an idea of what to expect, nothing could have prepared me for the actual experience of the lights, the crowds of people, and chaotic energy of Times Square. I felt that same sense of awe that I had experienced as a little girl visiting our

Dad and me in the Big Apple.

nation's capital. I could never have imagined then that because of the show, I would soon be traveling all over the country, speaking to young people about my experience as a teen mom.

I am fortunate to have been to pretty much every big city in the US (Los Angeles, Dallas, Miami, Denver, Charlotte, St. Louis, Orlando, and Las Vegas to name a few) but what I have really loved are all the opportunities I have had to visit small towns all over the South, the Midwest, and the Northeast. At first, when I would travel to a speaking engagement, I would go straight from the airport, to the venue, to a hotel, and then back to the airport. I never got to see the places I was visiting, and it felt like I could have been anywhere.

Perhaps travel cannot prevent bigotry, but by demonstrating that all peoples cry, laugh, eat, worry, and die, it can introduce the idea that if we try and understand each other, we may even become friends.

–Maya Angelou

After about a year, I decided to start renting a car. Now, whenever I travel to a new town or city and I have a spare hour or two, I just drive around on my own and take in the local landscape. There's nothing quite like the freedom you feel behind the wheel of a car, exploring the back roads of the countryside, or the mountains. These moments feed my soul and remind me of all the blessings in my life.

LIFE LESSONS

In recent years, psychologists and neuroscientists have begun examining more closely what many people have already learned anecdotally: that **spending time abroad** may have the potential to **affect mental change**. In general, creativity is related to neuroplasticity, or how the brain is wired. Neural pathways are influenced by environment and habit, meaning they're also sensitive to change: New sounds, smells, language, tastes, sensations, and sights spark different synapses in the brain and may have the potential to **revitalize the mind**.

Source: The Atlantic, March 31, 2015

My mom and I ham it up in one of London's iconic "red telephone boxes."

Take Your Vacation Days!

Although the benefits of travel may seem obvious, recent studies have shown that, although nearly three-quarters of Americans earn paid time off, more and more people are giving up their paid vacations days, opting instead to work months on end to meet deadlines and prove company loyalty.

However, while corporations and upper management may or may not appreciate your dedication to the job, not taking vacation days has been shown to decrease a person's productivity and work performance. On the other hand, taking time off to travel is food for the soul and can have the following benefits:

- **Broadens your mind:** Experiencing new cultures, meeting new people, and trying exotic new foods expands your experience and opens your mind to new ideas.

- **New perspective:** Traveling forces us to temporarily disconnect from our daily lives, which in turn gives us greater perspective and helps us appreciate the people and things we have in life.

- **Increases creativity:** More and more studies are showing that getting out of your comfort zone sparks creativity. Many doctors believe that experiencing new places helps develop new neural connections that trigger original and creative thoughts.

- **Increases self-confidence:** There's nothing quite like the feeling that comes from mastering the subway system in a new city, or successfully ordering food in another language. Being in a place where you do not know anyone and therefore must fend for yourself increases your ability to cope with obstacles, which in turn makes you a confident person and helps you grow as a person.

- **Self-discovery:** How well, or not so well, you navigate situations that you wouldn't ordinarily experience in your daily life leads to a greater understanding of one's self and what you are capable of.

- **Priceless memories:** Traveling with friends or family helps you build stronger bonds and creates precious memories that will last a lifetime.

For our honeymoon, Taylor and I made the decision to leave the kids with my parents and take some time on our own at a resort in Grenada. I had never been apart from my children for that long, so it wasn't easy to leave them, but we knew it was important for us to take that time together after our wedding. Once the guilt and worry settled down, we were able to leave behind all the stress and pressure of parenthood and just be two people in love, having adventures and enjoying one another's company.

We rented a 4-wheel drive Razor—which is kind of like a dune buggy—and left the resort to explore the mountains and the mountain trails, and check out the waterfalls and hot springs. One Friday night we broke the rules and left the resort to go to a local bar, where we got to drink and laugh with some of the local people. We packed years' worth of experiences into those two weeks, which strengthened our bond in a way that no amount of time together at home would.

> *There was nowhere to go but everywhere,*
> *So just keep rolling under the stars.*
> —Jack Kerouac

LIFE LESSONS

In a study commissioned by **Project: Time Off** and conducted by Oxford Economics, **Americans fail to use 429 million vacation** days every year. If American workers used all of their available time off, the US economy could reap an additional $160 billion in total business sales each year, supporting 1.2 million new American jobs. Furthermore, this additional economic activity would generate more than $21 billion in taxes.

Source: projecttimeoff.com

Home Sweet Home

There's nothing quite like travel to make you appreciate home. As much as I enjoy traveling, I love that moment when I walk through my front door after being away for a few days, and I am greeted by the familiar sights, sounds, and smells of home. Traveling is amazing, but there's no place like home.

Journey Within

Finding the time—not to mention, the money—to travel around the country or abroad isn't always a realistic option, but there is another kind of travel that can be just as beneficial to your soul. Sometimes the challenges in your mind can be more significant than the physical challenges of travel. Taking time to explore your mind can be just as rejuvenating as a hike in the mountains or a day on the beach. Set aside a regular time to allow your mind to reflect, process, or even just wander:

- **Meditate:** More and more, meditation (spending time in quiet thought, or reflection) is being recognized as an effective way of reducing stress. It clears the mind, promotes wellness, and provides a much-needed escape from the pressures of daily life.

- **Read:** Just like every other muscle in your body, your brain needs regular exercise to stay healthy and strong. Not only can a well-written novel temporarily transport you to another world, reading daily provides the mental stimulation your brain needs to stay sharp and engaged.

- **Write:** Taking the time to articulate your thoughts and feelings into words helps organize disorganized thoughts into more cohesive ones that give meaning to our experiences.

- **Daydream:** Allowing your mind to drift and wander may seem pointless or childish, but taking a break from distractions and multitasking long enough to allow your stream of consciousness to kick in, makes room for inspiration and self-discovery.

Chapter 10

HONOR YOUR
FATHER AND MOTHER

*Start children off on the way they should go,
and even when they are old they will not turn
from it.*

–PROVERBS 22:6

No matter what challenge I face in life, I know that I
can always look to my family and our faith for guidance and support. Family and faith are at the core of who
I am and everything I do in life. To me, the two are interconnected; the values and principles I've learned from
our faith will always be reinforced by my family.

My dad grew up in a big extended family in the small
idyllic town of Sweetwater, Tennessee, most of whom still
live there. His family was, and still is, deeply connected
to the local church, a small, family-focused (formerly
Baptist) congregation that became non-denominational
a few years back to be more inclusive of the larger
community. Eight years ago, my grandfather took over
as preacher. At a typical service there are usually fifty to

sixty people who gather to observe, and I'm usually related to about two-thirds of them.

Some Sundays, my grandparents will arrive at the church early and go down to the basement, where there's a community kitchen, to cook breakfast for the entire congregation. Everyone is welcome and there's never any judgment. On any given Sunday, you'll see people dressed in their Sunday best and others in dirty blue jeans and work boots. There's always lots of singing; there's an open invitation for anyone to stand up and sing—and lots of people do. The choir is made up of the children in the congregation, and they sing at every service and put on plays at the holidays. Some of my favorite childhood memories are of Sundays spent with my dad's family in this church.

What I love most about my grandfather's church is that there is no fire and brimstone, no condemnation of sinners; it is an open, welcoming community that teaches the importance of family, community, faith, and worship though the lessons of the bible. Even though I am not an active member, I still attend services with Taylor from time to time, in hopes of passing these same values on to our children.

> *"Family is the most important thing in the world."*
> —Princess Diana

"Science is not only compatible with spirituality; it is a profound source of spirituality. When we recognize our place in an immensity of light-years and in the passage of ages, when we grasp the intricacy, beauty, and subtlety of life, then that soaring feeling, that sense of elation and humility combined, is surely spiritual. So are our emotions in the presence of great art or music or literature, or acts of exemplary selfless courage such as those of Mohandas Gandhi or Martin Luther King, Jr. The notion that science and spirituality are somehow mutually exclusive does a disservice to both."

—CARL SAGAN

S. B. N. R.

While I am not particularly religious, I am a spiritual person. My spirituality comes from a connectedness to my family and the values they have instilled in me; faith in God, confidence in myself, and respect for the world around me. More and more Americans, especially young people, are identifying as "Spiritual But Not Religious." But, what does this mean in today's world, and can "spirituality" take the place of organized religion in our lives? Much wiser and more qualified people than me have attempted to answer those questions, but I believe that being "religious" means that you follow and identify with the teachings of a particular institution (such as Christianity, Islam, or Judaism), whereas "spirituality" is a more individual path that focuses on the well-being and integration of mind, body, and spirit.

I was raised to believe that your relationship with God is personal, and that above all you must have faith in something greater than yourself, so that even at your lowest times you will know you are not alone. Even non-religious institutions like Alcoholics Anonymous and Narcotics Anonymous emphasize the importance of placing faith in a "higher power." For me that higher power comes from both my faith in God and my faith in family.

LIFE LESSONS

In a study conducted jointly with the PBS television program *Religion & Ethics NewsWeekly*, the **Pew Research Center's Forum on Religion & Public Life** reported in 2012 that:

- Many of the country's 46 million unaffiliated adults are **religious** or spiritual in some way.
- Two-thirds (68%) of them say they **believe in God**.
- More than half (58%) say they often feel a **deep connection with nature**.
- More than a third (37%) classify themselves as **"spiritual" but not "religious."**
- One-in-five (21%) say they **pray every day**.

Source: pewforum.org

Church of Baseball

In a world where we're more likely to communicate with one another through Facebook than face-to-face, it's more important than ever that we put down our cell phones, step outside, and connect with people *IRL*. For my dad and his family, the church isn't just a place of worship; it's a place where the community gathers together to celebrate family and life. Connectedness, to something greater than yourself, is an important part of spirituality, and finding what that connection might be is a very personal discovery. I've met people who have found it through ties to their culture, in school, or the arts, even through athletics.

Growing up, sports were huge for me and my brother. Baseball, softball, motocross, wrestling, volleyball—we had a sport for every season. Not only did being part of a team instill in us a sense of self-confidence and responsibility, it also united us as a family and created moments of total connectedness. My mom and dad spent hours every week driving us to and from our different practices, games, and out of town tournaments, and in those long car rides we would talk about anything and everything. If you've ever tried to ask a teenager directly what he or she did at school that day you will invariably be told "nothing" or "I dunno." Children are like skittish cats, if you come at them head-on they'll retreat. But, you'd be amazed how

> *"I believe in the church of baseball. I've tried all the major religions and most of the minor ones. I've worshipped Buddha, Allah, Brahma, Vishnu, Shiva, trees, mushrooms, and Isadora Duncan. I know things... I've tried them all, I really have. And, the only church that feeds the soul, day in, day out, is the church of baseball."*
>
> –SUSAN SARANDON, *BULL DURHAM*

much you can learn just from an hour of uninterrupted chitchat in the car.

Now that Bentley plays sports, Taylor has been coaching his baseball and basketball teams, and when Jayde and Maverick are old enough to play sports I'm sure we'll coach their teams as well. Anyone who has ever played, or had a kid who plays, *any* sport knows it is a huge time commitment. But if you love it, it's worth it because the experience instills in children (and adults) a sense of belonging and responsibility to a larger community, something greater than oneself that is organized around a set of shared values and goals.

Family Ties

My brother and I have always had a close relationship with our parents. Growing up, we spent a lot of time together as a family. Between year-round sport commitments, family trips camping or to the beach, and the fact that my mom started working from home when I was in

A Bookout family rafting trip in 2012. In the front are my dad and Matt. Then me, my mom, and Matt's then-girlfriend, Megan. The guy in the back was our raft guide. His name was Todd but he told us people call him "Re-Todd."

middle school (so she was always there when my brother and I got home from school), our parents were a constant presence in our lives. Who my brother and I have become as adults is a direct result of our parents' involvement in our lives and the importance they placed on family.

Even though I didn't necessarily understand this growing up, I always knew that no matter what, my family had my back. There's no blame, no judgment, just reassurance and support. That's not to say we don't call each other on our shit, or point out when we're making mistakes. Our thing is: "I've got your back now, but if you're being an idiot I'm gonna let you know later." We always put family first, and we will always be there for each other. Now that I have children of my own, I truly understand the importance of a strong family foundation in their development.

LIFE LESSONS

Spending time together as a family also has many **positive developmental** impacts, including:

- Increased language development
- Greater sense of self
- Feelings of love and acceptance
- Enhanced thinking and reasoning skills
- An understanding of family values
- Increased respect for others

Source: mommyunivercitynj.org

The Grandfather Clause

My relationship with my mom hasn't changed much over the years. She's my hero, my rock, and my best friend—and she always has been. My relationship with my dad, however, got a lot stronger after Bentley was born. As a teenager I didn't have a lot of common ground with him, but once I had a child (and became an adult overnight) we developed a mutual respect that hadn't really been there before. We were able to appreciate each other and even admire some of the traits that drove us crazy about one another when I was a kid.

One thing I've observed with *all* the men in my children's lives (my dad, Ryan's dad, Taylor's dad) is that when they have grandchildren they soften up. I think it has to do with the fact that they aren't responsible for raising that child, so they're able to tap into their emotional side in a way that they weren't when their own kids were growing up.

Gene's Gems

My dad has a very unique way of looking at the world and he's not at all shy about dispensing his particular brand of wisdom. I always joke that I want to start

> *"The one mistake I made was thinking I was wrong."*
> −GENE BOOKOUT

a Twitter account for him and call it "Shit Gene Says." I get my extreme sense of loyalty from my dad. If it's 3:00 a.m. and I have a flat tire, there are only one or two people I would call (and one of them is my dad). On the other hand, I'm on twenty people's list. I get that from my father. He's everybody's go-to guy. He has a moral compass that points true north. His loyalty and generosity aren't always reciprocated, but instead of being bitter or becoming cynical about it, he uses humor to remind people to be true to their word.

1. **"If you have to borrow something more than twice, you should buy your own."** This one he says to my brother and me just about every other week.

2. **"It's better to have it and not need it, than to need it and not have it."** (I've always taken this one to heart. I am always cold, so if I go somewhere for more than thirty-five minutes, I always bring a sweater.)

3. **"It's better to be thought a fool, than to open your mouth and remove all doubt."** (If ya'll can't interpret that one, there's no hope for you.)

4. **"Never look a gift horse in the mouth."** My dad always said this when we were kids and I never understood it. Then one day he explained to me that horses' teeth grow over time, so checking their length is a way of gauging old age, and therefore a sign of mistrust towards the giver. An example of this is when my car had to be repaired and my dad lent me one from his shop that he was planning to fix up and resell. After driving the car for less than a day, I realized it had some quirky issues (like the darned thing would automatically lock me out if the door shut while it was still running), but despite the aggravation I was never ungrateful because he was doing me a favor by letting me borrow the car for free.

5. **"Y'all are so lucky."** My dad loves to set people up with this line. Now my brother, mom, and I know not

to ask, "Why?" But he can usually find some unsus-
pecting victim to take the bait and then he'll respond,
"Because you can kiss my ass and I can't."

6. If somebody seems a little too overconfident that
they are going to do something, my dad will respond,
**"You don't have the hair on your ass if you don't do
it."** *Translation:* Be true to your word.

7. **"Hurray for me and to hell with you."** Say you're on
a boat and the boat's sinking and there's one lifeboat.
If you choose to save yourself and abandon the rest
of the passengers, "Hurray for me and to hell with
you," is what my dad would have you saying. It's his
favorite expression and it's not something you ever
want to be guilty of.

8. **"If I tell you it's Christmas time that means Santa's
coming."** This means I'm true to my word, and you
can bank on it.

9. When my dad says goodbye to people he usually says
one of two things. If someone says, "It was so good to
see you," my dad will respond, **"I'm so glad you got to
see me, too."** Or, as he's shaking your hand he'll say,
"Okay, if you need me, I'll call ya."

10. **"It's like a one-legged man in an ass-kicking
contest."** Some people may take offense at this one
because they will assume it's about being useless. But
for my dad this expression has two other completely

different meanings. When someone has to face an obstacle in life, but it's clear to my dad things are not going to work out the way that person hoped, this is my dad's way of saying maybe you're overshooting here. The other meaning is that if a one-legged person enters an ass-kicking contest then they're probably going to win because they're already kicking ass all day every day. So, in this case, it means don't doubt yourself.

She Thinks We're Just Fishin'

My great-grandfather was the patriarch of the Bookout family. Growing up, my brother and I spent a lot of time on his farm. Even though we were little and probably not much use to him, my grandfather always took us along when he did chores on the farm. We'd pick green beans or potatoes from my great-grandmother's garden and prep them for dinner. Or help him with the horses and the stables, grooming them or putting food in their feeders. At the time I didn't think too deeply about it. I just picked the vegetables or fed the horses and chatted with my great-granddad.

It wasn't until years later, after he died, that it finally dawned on me *why* he always took us along. I was listening to "Just Fishin'" by country music singer Trace Adkins and in the song a father takes his little girl

"In the end, that's what being a parent is all about—those precious moments with our children that fill us with pride and excitement for their future, the chances we have to set an example or offer a piece of advice, the opportunities to just be there and show them that we love them."

—BARACK OBAMA

fishing. While she's thinking about what they're going to catch, he knows that what they're really doing is building memories that will last her a lifetime. That's what my great-granddad was doing. He took us along, not because we were in any way useful to him on the farm, but to teach us in his subtle way about independence, while strengthening our bond with him and giving us memories that I will cherish for the rest of my life.

BEYOND
BULLETPROOF

If there's one thing I regret from this crazy, challenging, totally unexpected and blessed life I've led, is that I ever gave anyone the impression that any of it was easy. It wasn't. I've made so many mistakes in my life, many of them under the scrutiny of a brutally critical public eye, but I've worked hard to make something of my life. I've stumbled more times than I can remember along my journey, but I always get back up and I keep moving forward. What I learned from the values my parents instilled in me is that I can let my mistakes define me, or I can learn from them and turn my struggles into strength.

What has kept me sane and grounded on this wild, unpredictable ride I stepped onto at the age of sixteen is that I *know* who I am. I've built a family, a marriage, a business; and I decided long ago never to let anyone else define me. Independence, personal expression, friendship, motherhood, love, family, and faith; these are essential components of who I am and how I've learned to be strong. The trick is creating a balance in your life for what truly matters to you. And the most important thing is to love yourself enough to make the right choices for your future.

I don't claim to have all the answers. In many ways I'm still that seventeen-year-old girl standing on the podium in front of a room full of strangers. Some things I've got worked out, others I'm still figuring out along the way. But if what I have learned can help just one person, then that's a little bit of light I've brought into the world. Being bulletproof isn't just about deflecting hate, it's about being strong enough to allow yourself to feel; to be vulnerable enough to let love in.

ABOUT THE AUTHOR

Maci Bookout starred on the MTV reality TV show *16 & Pregnant* and went on to become a fan favorite on the spin-off *Teen Mom.* Known for her down-to-earth Southern charm and level-headed personality, Maci has earned the respect of teens and adults alike with her courage under pressure and her mature reflections on teen pregnancy and motherhood. Maci has appeared on numerous talk shows and spoken to many educational groups on teen pregnancy prevention. She consistently receives praise from the audience for her candidness, down to earth personality, and refreshingly insightful commentary. Maci also makes personal appearances at marketing/ promotional events, keynote speeches, colleges, TV shows, sporting events, and other unique spokesperson/ appearance opportunities. In addition to being a public speaker, writer, and tv/radio host, Maci is a mom to three children and recently married Taylor McKinney.